NOTHING LEFT BUT FOOTPRINTS

NOTHING LEFT BUT FOOTPRINTS

Hazel Nicholson

The Book Guild Ltd
Sussex, England

To Ian, Anthony and Fiona
who made it all possible

The Book Guild Ltd,
25 High Street,
Lewes, Sussex

First published 1996
© Hazel Nicholson, 1996
Set in Times
Typesetting by Raven Typesetters, Chester

Printed in Great Britain by
Bookcraft (Bath) Ltd

A catalogue record for this book is
available from the British Library

ISBN 1 85776 091 3

1

One wintry morning during the 1970s an airmail letter arrived, bearing a Zambian postmark. It was addressed to my husband, Ian, who slipped it into his pocket as he left the house, leaving me consumed with curiosity. At the time, neither of us realised just how much the contents of the letter would alter the course of our lives.

Returning home that evening, Ian mentioned casually that he had heard from Charles Lang, a friend of long standing. Recently promoted to general manager of a motor company, he was considering replacing the chief accountant, and wondered if Ian would be interested in filling the position.

Charles and my husband arranged to meet towards the end of May. In the meantime Ian, fired with enthusiasm, could talk of little else, dismissing any reservations on my part. Although I was not completely adverse to the idea, I had mixed feelings about spreading my wings so soon after moving to Somerset, which in itself had been quite an upheaval. Apart from that, I was still very much under the spell of the surrounding countryside.

Studying the map of Africa, I located Zambia, in the shape of a developing foetus, wedged between Malawi and Angola. A trip to the local reference library proved to be most fruitful. Once I had scratched the surface I started to conjure up glorious visits to the Victoria Falls along with exciting excursions to various game parks. On the way home, I visualised myself developing a golden tan as I sunbathed on the shores of Lake Kariba and other such exotic locations.

During Charles's brief visit, when all the finer details were discussed, it was decided that Ian would take up his new appointment at the beginning of August. From then onwards life took on a new meaning as we rushed around making all the necessary preparations. Some of these proved to be less than inspiring. This included being immunised against such formidable diseases as smallpox and yellow fever.

Ian wasn't at all deterred by well-meaning friends who persisted in bringing to our attention some of the atrocities which, they stipulated, were rampant in that part of the world. 'According to the law of averages, there's far more likelihood of our being run over by a bus in the high street,' my husband responded nonchalantly.

Just when we thought we had solved all our immediate problems, we were faced with the dilemma of whether or not to part with Jojo, the family cat. I half-heartedly asked around, but nobody wanted an eleven-year-old tabby without any form of pedigree. 'I hate all cats,' was my sister's response, upon being approached. After further debate, we placed an order with a local firm for a suitable container in which Jojo might tackle the journey in relative comfort.

On the day of our departure, filling the litter tray perhaps a little too liberally, I placed the cat gently inside the basket before carefully securing the lid. To my astonishment, at the airport check-in I was informed that the container, termed as excessive baggage, was grossly overweight. Aware that there was no alternative, I submissively handed over the exorbitant fee demanded.

Upon landing at Lusaka Airport our arrival was far from welcoming. The officials appeared arrogant and aloof as they ushered us from one department to another. Innumerable forms had to be filled in and various documents produced, none of which seemed to be quite in order. We were eventually informed that our connecting flight to the Copperbelt had been delayed, which we later learned was the rule rather than the exception!

Any optimistic feelings I might still have harboured after our reception in Lusaka evaporated completely as our plane taxied to a standstill at Southdown Airport, on the outskirts of Kitwe.

Emerging from the aircraft my heart sank. The word primitive describes aptly the large single-storeyed building into which we were shepherded. This housed the reception and customs areas, and was expected to cater to all our needs. Any calls of nature were best ignored due to the state of the plumbing. Once we had taken care of the necessary formalities, much to our relief, our luggage put in an appearance, as did David Roberts, who had arranged to meet us.

Jolting along the narrow tarmac, which seemed in no particular hurry to join the main Kitwe highway, I made every effort to appear interested in my surroundings. Although this was not our first visit to the Continent, I had never seriously contemplated raising a family in the heart of Africa. Under the circumstances I felt I could be excused for feeling less than optimistic. The children, Anthony and Fiona, much to their credit, seemed to take all in their stride.

Along the way David kept up a running commentary, answering most of our queries with forbearance. For the first few miles we drove through scrubland, passing a number of sprawling villages. One-roomed, conical-shaped mud huts with thatched roofs caught and held our attention. David explained how each unit housed a complete family, which made me wonder how even the smallest household managed to cope in such cramped conditions. The chief, as a status symbol, often preferred to live in a brick-built construction with a corrugated iron roof.

Chickens and goats were stabled in miniature rondavals, erected on wooden stilts raised high above the ground, presumably for reasons of security. Some evidence of agriculture formed a perimeter fence. This consisted mostly of yellow flowering tomato plants, dwarfed by rows of mealies and clumps of banana and pawpaw trees.

Without warning the tarmac suddenly forked right, forming a junction with the main highway. From here onwards I relaxed considerably. The climate could only be described as idyllic, as a benevolent sun shone down from the bluest of skies, revitalising my travel-weary spirits.

We learned that the local inhabitants belonged mainly to the Bember tribe. I noticed that the young men were dressed no differently from their contemporaries in the West. They too had joined the blue jeans brigade, strutting along in wide flares and high-heeled boots. The women wore the most colourful crimplene dresses and some carried a chitengi cloth. By tradition this serves as a long skirt or shawl with which a mother would secure an infant to her back. Nowadays, however, the less maternal, more fashion-conscious female has it at the ready to wrap around mini-skirted legs, should propriety demand!

Every few miles, propped up at the side of the road, crudely constructed notices were to be seen, advertising 'The Wire Bicycle Company of Zambia.' Nearby, neatly laid out rows of miniature bikes, in a variety of sizes, were on display. Each tiny wheel had been bound painstakingly in strips of rubber, taken from vehicles which,

7

when they expired, were abandoned along the highway.

Every now and then we could not help but smile at the antics of groups of cheerful youths who had set up souvenir stalls and were equally determined to attract the attention of passing motorists. Each fleeting scene added a touch of colour to what could be described as an unexciting landscape.

David slowed down in order that we could get a better view of the assortment of merchandise on offer. Tempting all but the most thrifty, highly polished figures sculptured out of malachite, wood and ivory, competed against colourful paintings and skilfully woven wicker bric-à-brac.

Before we knew it, we had crossed the three sets of railway lines used to transport wagonloads of copper from the mines. Joining the flow of traffic travelling along Independence Avenue, we headed towards the centre of Kitwe, branching off into President Avenue, just before the main convoy reached Kaunda Square.

Lechwe Motors was our immediate destination. Charles Lang was still overseas on business at the time. Having been forewarned of numerous shortages, due to a flagging economy, we didn't quite know what to expect, so kept an open mind. The Range Rover eventually stopped outside a garage and well-stocked showroom with a large office block to the rear. At a glance one could see the place was well-maintained, which cheered our spirits immensely.

When Charles had invited my husband to join the company, a substantial increase in salary and generous perks had mainly influenced his decision to accept. As far as I was concerned, although at first less than enthusiastic, the promise of a spacious house with swimming pool had been a definite vote winner.

Charles and Ian had become firm friends when they were articled clerks to a firm of accountants during the fifties. They had lost contact with one another after taking their finals, when Charles emigrated to South Africa. By pure coincidence, they were reunited several years later when they were posted to Kamasi, the 'Garden City' of Ghana. Unfortunately, eighteen months later, a family tragedy forced Charles to break his contract with the firm and return south. The following autumn Ian also resigned, taking up an appointment near Reading. From then onwards they saw little of one another but corresponded fairly regularly.

8

At that time I was employed by a high street bank in Reading town centre. Sometimes joining a group of colleagues, I would pop over to the Friars' Tea Bar during my lunch break. It was there that I first met Ian. Catching his eye I smiled at him, whereupon, to his mortification, he upset the cup he was carrying, splashing me in the process. As far as I was concerned, it was love at first sight; well worth all the disruption that ensued!

The first person to whom we were introduced at Lechwe Motors was Grace Shaw, the company secretary. While we were in her office several other members of staff popped in to greet us. These included Paul Drake who, we gathered at the time, was quite unaware that he was about to become my husband's predecessor. I think he must have sensed something unpleasant was pending, for he seemed full of doom and gloom about life in general.

Later Grace mentioned that Paul's wife had left him recently for someone with whom she had been having an affair. I got the distinct impression that Grace had little if any sympathy for Paul, being of the opinion that he had brought his misfortunes upon himself. At the time I was appalled by her heartless attitude, but soon discovered that there might have been more than an element of truth in her observations.

Later that morning David invited us to accompany him to lunch at the Kitwe Club. Well aware that standards might differ somewhat from those in the West, I was nevertheless ill-prepared for the air of dilapidation that engulfed the interior of the clubhouse. Alcohol, fortunately, did not appear to be in short supply, so bidding the children to play outside on the swings for a while, I joined David and Ian in the bar for a refreshing gin and tonic.

The restaurant at that time was known as The Fox's Hole. Although the decor was tatty, the atmosphere was most welcoming. A smiling waiter showed us to a table on the shaded verandah, at the far end of the room. While the chef grilled generous-sized portions of steak over a charcoal fire, we helped ourselves from a wide assortment of salads and sauces, displayed attractively on a circular table. The meal proved to be delicious and Anthony and Fiona, slightly overawed, helped to add to our enjoyment by behaving angelically.

A few months later we applied to become members of the club, by then quite oblivious to the shabby surroundings. Here we spent many happy hours, taking part in various activities and enjoying the convivial atmosphere of the lounge bar.

As we left the Kitwe Club that afternoon David informed us that he had asked Grace to take me on a tour of the town centre. Accompanied by the children, the first place we visited was CBC, a supermarket in the main shopping area. At a glance it was fairly obvious that provisions in the grocery section were in very short supply. By comparison, however, the fancy goods department displayed a vast array of copperware, which rubbed shoulders with numerous rows of shoes and various items of clothing and cosmetics.

The only other shop of any magnitude was ZOK, a large cooperative. That afternoon an endless queue formed outside the store as rumour spread that some much sought-after commodity had became available.

After Independence, in October 1964, a large number of establishments had been taken over by the Asian community. It was generally accepted that the local Africans were not shopkeepers by nature as they viewed with antipathy the very idea of ploughing any profit back into the business.

No bond of friendship was forged between Grace and myself that afternoon. Instead, I got the distinct impression that showing me around was one chore she could have done without. She failed completely to disguise the fact that she was more than eager to return to her place of employment. At the time, feeling somewhat dejected, I purchased a few essentials, deciding to do the bulk of my shopping later with Ian, whose company I knew would be far more congenial.

Upon our return I turned to thank Grace but need not have bothered, for she was already making a beeline for the stairs. However, the receptionist who was chatting to David at the time, was far more cordial. She invited me to try on an intricately carved ivory bracelet, given to her as a birthday present. I could not help but admire it, even though well aware that trading in ivory encouraged poaching, which was strictly taboo.

Ian and I gathered from David that we were to stay in the company's transit flat over the next few weeks or at least until Paul moved out of the bungalow which was eventually to be our new home. Although not luxurious by any standards, our temporary accommodation was fairly large and adequately furnished. It normally housed new employees until something more permanent could be found. The servants' quarters were situated across the yard from the flat. When showing us around David startled everyone by summoning Bernard, the houseboy, at the top of his voice, from the kitchen veranda.

Although we were practically deafened, Bernard apparently heard not a sound. Later, however, he deigned to put in an appearance. Upon being informed that Ian was to be his new bwana for a while, he scowled and said nothing. I was in the process of offering him my hand but thought better of it, allowing my arm to return limply to my side. At that moment my little home in England seemed such a long way away, and suddenly I missed the security I had, inevitably, abandoned.

2

During their last reunion Charles mentioned that David Roberts had recently been recruited as showroom manager. It was, therefore, not surprising that Ian was a trifle confused when summoned to David's office one morning. Itemising various rules and regulations, David reiterated that, whilst he held the reins, members of staff, including the chief accountant, should be punctual and arrive on time each day. Deciding to humour his colleague for the time being, Ian took David's bombastic attitude in his stride.

Fortunately, this state of affairs did not last for long. Returning from overseas, Charles clarified the situation by explaining that any seniority on David's part was by virtue of his grey hair alone! In all fairness, I must admit that although David could be infuriating at times, in general he was extremely charming. Rumour had it that in some quarters he was, in fact, considered to be quite a lady-killer!

Until Ian received his first pay cheque towards the end of August we had very little money to spend on anything but the bare necessities. Not wishing to exchange precious sterling for kwatcha, we entertained as little as possible and seldom went anywhere. If on the rare occasion we felt obliged to do so I usually asked Bernard's wife Jolita to baby-sit. For this service we paid her most handsomely. This proved to be no sweetener, however, for her attitude towards me was and continued to be little less than hostile. Fortunately, the children accepted the couple philosophically. Anthony would often keep us amused by relating anecdotes that had taken place during our absence. 'Jolita is really quite nice,' he explained on one occasion when he overheard me complaining. 'I wish she wouldn't keep carrying me about on her back though. When I ask her to put me down she just won't listen.' This was followed shortly with the observation, 'You know what, Mummy, Bernard and Jolita never really get cross with us, no matter how naughty Fiona is!'

Pay day arrived at last and from then onwards the quality of our lives improved considerably. Taking Charles's advice, we became members of the local boating club which certainly proved to be a step in the right direction.Whenever we spent an evening there we were able to take the children with us. If it happened to be well past their bedtime before we left they would find a large comfortable armchair in which to curl up and fall asleep. This appeared to have no adverse effect on their wellbeing, but I was quite aware that there were those who disapproved of our 'bohemian ways'.

Shortly after moving into the transit flat we were invited to dinner by Jade and Ivor Coetzee, a couple from Natal. Ivor was employed as a salesman at Lechwe Motors, where he was nicknamed Ivor the Skiver. This description was far from apt when it came to entertaining, however, for he spared no time or effort in making sure his guests enjoyed themselves.

On the evening in question we had only been there for what seemed like a matter of minutes, however, when without warning the burglar alarm went off, startling everyone present. Ivor, who went immediately to investigate, returned shortly, reassuring his guests that there was really no cause for concern. It emerged that the older children had been permitted to watch television for a while in their parents' bedroom. One of them had mistakenly turned on the alarm instead of the light switch, resulting in bedlam.

When peace reigned once more Jade confided that only three of her five children were fathered by Ivan. The remaining two were the offspring of two previous partners. To add to the population explosion, Ivor had four children by two former wives who had remarried and produced several more, making a baker's dozen in all. From all the commotion some minutes earlier, I imagined that the entire family tree must have been present that evening.

During the following months I became quite friendly with various members of this extended family, who kept in close contact and got along splendidly with one another most of the time. So much so, in fact, that there were moments when one was inclined to wonder just who belonged to whom. This applied not only to the offspring, but fortunately, no one seemed to make an issue out of it.

Having enjoyed an excellent meal which I felt threatened my own limited culinary efforts, we adjourned to the front room for coffee. As Ivor handed me a liqueur he inquired if I was enjoying life in

Africa. I replied that apart from the massive spiders that clung to the ceiling above our beds, and those revolting giant cockroaches which flew in at the open window without warning, I found it quite agreeable. I stressed, however, that I couldn't wait to move into Paul's bungalow.

'What have you got against the transit flat?' Jade queried.

'Well for starters, only an idiot would have chosen white tiles for a kitchen floor,' I objected, adding, 'Whoever was responsible for laying them must have had more than their fair share of alcohol at the time.'

Ivor roared with laughter before admitting that he was the culprit and could well have been 'on his ear'. He then went on to explain that Jade and he had lived there when they first got married, before the company took it over. Not long after moving in they had decided to hold a surprise party for their friends. The surprise turned out to be that as each guest arrived they were handed a drink and pile of floor tiles, complete with instructions. What was even more surprising was the fact that the whole task had been completed by the time the party broke up the following day. 'They did a splendid job,' Ivan concluded, with a faraway look in his eyes. When I attempted to apologise for any lack of tact on my part, my words were drowned by good-humoured banter.

When the Coetzees returned to live in South Africa they were greatly missed by all who knew them, even though their lifestyle was often considered to be socially unconventional. After they had vacated their home, which was company property, I accompanied Ian when he visited the premises to take an inventory. On a pile of discarded bric-à-brac, I spotted a small carving of a kudu. It was perfect in every detail, apart from the left ear which had a minute chip in it. Retrieving the statue, I took it with me when we left. To this day, I cannot look at the carving without remembering all the happy hours we spent in the company of the Coetzees and their extended family. Although we lost touch with them with the passing of time, their charming and winning ways made our lives richer for having known them.

We must have been living in the transit flat for about a month when Charles returned to Zambia. He arrived unaccompanied as a broken wrist had prevented his wife, Sofia, from travelling with him. I heard through the grapevine that she had been twirled off her feet whilst taking part in a display of Scottish dancing. Still suffering a certain amount of discomfort from her injuries, she had decided to delay her return for a few weeks.

Under the circumstances, Ian thought it would be a welcoming gesture to invite Charles to dine with us on his first night back. I am sure my husband's intentions were most admirable. Unfortunately, he failed to give me prior warning, with the result that I found myself in something of a quandary when the two men arrived, unannounced, on the doorstep that evening.

Due to the tightness of our budget during that period, I made do with the bare necessities and shopped for food on a daily basis. Praying for a miracle, I examined the contents of the refrigerator, in vain. As the children had already had their supper, all I found were the two small chops and some vegetables which I had intended to cook for the two of us that night. Making a snap decision, I dashed downstairs to the Paynes' flat which was on the floor below.

We had been introduced to Beth and her husband, Tom Payne – a motor mechanic, employed by Lechwe Motors – on what could only be described as a far from happy occasion. They were feeling extremely dejected at the time, having just returned from an appointment with an ophthalmologist in Salisbury. It transpired that their suspicions that their baby daughter, Lisa, was going blind, had been confirmed. At the same time any hope that an operation might improve her vision had been dispelled.

Much to their credit, they did not dwell too deeply on their daughter's handicap. In all other ways Lisa was the perfect baby. We watched her grow into a delightful littler toddler, gurgling and chuckling happily as she stumbled from one piece of furniture to another in her determination to become mobile.

Bursting in on the Paynes that evening, I briefly explained my predicament, imploring Beth for some assistance. As fate would have it, they appeared to be equally as impatient for pay day to arrive. Beth, however, immediately offered me some of the pork sausages she was in the process of preparing for their evening meal. These I accepted with gratitude, making a mental note to repay such generosity as soon as possible, with interest.

Aware that such meagre rations would not stretch to satisfying the appetites of three healthy adults, I set the dining room table for two. In order to save face, I feigned to be suffering from a slight bout of colic. Ian was most attentive and to help settle my upset stomach poured me out a stiff brandy. Meanwhile, our guest, quite unaware that he was the cause of my sudden affliction, sympathised dutifully. Both men then proceeded to tuck into the meal with great relish, while my only source of sustenance, that evening, came out of a bottle!

3

Any anxiety on my part concerning Jojo's wellbeing was soon dispelled. Finally liberated, she emerged like a seasoned traveller, eager to inspect her new surroundings and none the worse for the experience. She settled into the transit flat from the start and a few weeks later accepted the move to the bungalow in Riverside without protest.

For a while her life seemed to be as near perfect as possible. The situation, unfortunately, began to deteriorate from the moment Paul, the previous occupier, arrived on our doorstep. Apparently he was having his work cut out trying to find a good home for his Rhodesian ridgeback, Amber. Regarding the massive creature with apprehension, I was far from surprised.

The animal had immediately fallen from grace by indiscriminately marking what she considered to be her territory. Seeing my expression of disapproval, Paul had attempted to appeal to my better nature. 'You are my last resort,' he pleaded. 'It would be tragic if I should have to have the dog destroyed, she is such a gentle, friendly, creature.'

Unable to resist either pair of appealing brown eyes, I finally agreed to provide temporary accommodation for the dog until a new owner materialised. At this Paul's attitude changed perceptively. He enquired cheerfully if I would consider buying some household items he no longer required. Before I realised it, he had charmed me into buying several pieces of furniture along with some oddments. His parting shot was, 'By the way, I will have to charge you a little something for the dog's collar and lead, they're real leather you understand!'

Once we became accustomed to Amber's strange ways we grew extremely fond of her, and she repaid our hospitality with an abundance of love and affection. Furthermore, she proved to be an excellent guard dog. At first we had made a half-hearted attempt to find her a new home but as none was forthcoming she eventually took up permanent residence with us.

From the onset, dog and cat became sworn enemies. Well out of reach, on the top of a cupboard, Jojo would arrogantly observe her aggressor, stretched out on the cool floor tiles below. The instant the cat showed the slightest sign of descending from her perch, the long knotted ridge along Amber's back would stand erect, as she prepared to do battle. Escaping through the kitchen door, Jojo would take refuge in a pawpaw tree which grew alongside the house. Bored with taunting the dog, she would eventually leap onto the roof and make her way to a favourite spot by the chimney, to shade from the sun's strong rays. Here she would stay until the irresistible aroma of Kapenta and mealie meal, simmering on the stove, compelled her to return for sustenance.

I imagine that during this period Jojo must have used up most of her nine lives. One fateful day she lost her footing and fell out of the pawpaw tree, to be immediately mauled by the pair of hungry jaws waiting below. Due to the patience and skill of the local vet, she managed to survive the ordeal. Nevertheless, it was obvious that the time had come to separate the two animals on a permanent basis.

In desperation, we mentioned our problem to the vet who promised to see what he could do. Eventually, he put us in touch with a farmer living across the border in Zaire, who was looking for a reliable guard dog. Watching Amber being driven away proved to be a heartbreaking experience. While my head told me I had made a wise decision, my heart was not at all convinced. The cruellest blow of all, however, was yet to come. Two days after Amber's departure, Jojo vanished. At first I was unconcerned, as it was not the first time she had deserted us for a day or two. When a week passed without sight or sound of her my anxiety turned to despair and I spent hours touring the neighbourhood, imploring our pet to return home.

I was horrified when some heartless person pointed out that there was little chance of my seeing Jojo again. 'Members of a local political persuasion manufacture their Davy Crocket style caps out of cats' fur, which they don with pride at party gatherings,' he elaborated callously. After that I resigned myself to the fact that Jojo was gone forever, comforting myself with the thought that she could well have found herself a 'safe house' to live in.

All was not lost, however, for some months later, as I opened the front door, I was confronted by Amber sitting patiently on the welcome mat. The poor creature was in a most pitiful state. Her once sleek coat was now dull and matted, looking far too large for her undernourished body. We immediately contacted the vet who examined the dog meticulously. A tendon in her back leg was badly swollen and she was suffering from tick fever which is, more often than not, fatal. He assured us, however, that with careful feeding and loving attention there was a possibility she might recover. He also promised to contact her present owner for further information.

It transpired that the dog had been missing for weeks. She had escaped from the farmer's pick-up while he was delivering some produce to the local market. He had left her in the cab with the window open a fraction and was amazed, upon his return, to find she had disappeared. 'If you want my opinion, that dog is not to be trusted and should be destroyed,' he then informed the vet, adding that she had already been replaced by a reliable Alsatian.

The next few weeks were touch and go as Amber's condition deteriorated. At times even the vet seemed to lose hope. I could not bear the thought of losing her again; this time most certainly forever.

I am convinced she would not have survived if it had not been for Benson, an elderly African who did odd jobs for us around the garden. On more than one occasion he had attempted to persuade me to visit the local witch doctor, a suggestion which I at first considered to be ludicrous and quite out of the question.

The witch doctor lived in a small hut along the Chingola Road. For a small sum he handed me a beer bottle containing some dubious-looking substance. 'Make sure the animal drinks some every day until the moon is round,' he insisted. This I did religiously.

'All's well that ends well,' I heard the vet murmur, as he examined Amber before finally pronouncing her fully recovered. Admiring her now lustrous eyes and gleaming coat, I gazed upon her with affection as she lay on the kitchen floor, wagging her tail contentedly.

My eyes strayed automatically to the shelf which had once been a haven for Jojo. Immediately I pictured her preening herself with one eye ever watchful. 'Who knows?' I thought wistfully. 'Perhaps there's still a chance she might return one day.'

Sadly she was never seen again.

4

Plans for our pool were still at the drawing board stage when we first moved to Orange Crescent. Having nothing better to do, the children and I would while away the afternoon swimming and sunbathing at the boating club. Situated on the bank of the Mindola dam, the clubhouse had originally been built much closer to the water, but relocated some years later when it was discovered to be sinking slowly into the surrounding slimes. Until I became the proud owner of a yellow VW Beetle Ian would drive the children and me there, before returning to work after lunch. Beth and her two small daughters usually accompanied us on these jaunts, which proved to be great fun.

I can recall my first visit to the dam as if it were yesterday. Driving along the airport road, through the trees on our left the Rhokana Golf Club was barely visible. Further on, branching off to the right, we drove across flat scrubland until a sharp left-hand bend led us down a short dirt track. Forking to the right at a small intersection, we jolted down a sandy slope for a hundred yards before arriving at the main gates.

Once inside, the inviting sparkling water reflected the mood of the day. Dotted around the jetty a motley array of sailing boats strained against their rigging, eager to be off scudding along in the breeze. Where the eucalyptus failed to offer much protection, wooden tables and benches, attractively shaded by large straw ceilings, were dotted around the grounds.

Ignoring the car park, void of any shelter to protect the car from the sun's blistering heat, Ian chose a spot behind the boathouse, under a clump of acacia trees. Before he had time to turn off the engine the children tumbled out, eager to get a closer view of what they considered was Paradise.

It did not take them long to locate the swimming pool, built on top of what had once been a gigantic ant hill. Beth and I went in search of the changing rooms where we hurriedly slipped into bikinis. We returned to find the children naked, having thrown all modesty aside. Impatiently, they clung to the railings, pleading with us to open the safety gate.

When we eventually saved enough to buy a small second-hand motor boat, we joined the power boat section and spent all our spare time learning to water ski, instructed by a group of Australians who had the patience of Job. Until then, we divided our attention between the rowing and sailing sections where a pair of spare hands was always welcome. Everyone seemed to congregate in the clubhouse after dark, so we soon got to know a large cross-section of the members.

Introduced to the dubious delights of jacks and fives, the children, who had previously shown little interest, became quite proficient at number work when rolling the dice.

It was during these sessions that we acquired our insatiable appetite for biltong. Although authentically prepared from long strips of venison, topside of beef was often used as a popular substitute. I discovered a simple recipe which consisted of rolling the meat in a concoction of saltpetre and various spices. It was then left for several days to dry out completely. In all honesty, however, mine never tasted so good as the delicious sticks sold over the clubhouse counter.

In the early seventies the majority of club members consisted mostly of expatriates, with a sprinkling of Rhodesians, South Africans and Brits who had stayed on after Independence. Expats like myself were nicknamed 'VC Tenners', after the mode of transport in which we had arrived. We put up with such jibes good-naturedly, and were eventually accepted by most if not all.

Upon returning home from the club one afternoon we were confronted by a gang of Africans digging up the front lawn. This certainly came as something of a surprise for, as far as I knew, no definite date had been set for work to start on the swimming pool. Neither the children nor I were able to control our excitement and delight at the prospect.

Beth and her children, who had accompanied us that afternoon, were invited to stay for tea. Our curiosity knew no bounds as everyone piled into Fiona's bedroom. An unobstructed view of the pro-

21

ceedings could be obtained from this vantage point, where we were able to watch behind shuttered windows without being observed.

A couple of Europeans were supervising a gang of African labourers. We learnt later that the elder of the two was a Dutchman named Karl Theron, the owner of the business. His assistant, Craig, was an extremely handsome young man who, regardless of his good looks, lacked both confidence and charm. Karl, on the other hand, possessed an abundance of both.

Karl and Craig spoke to the Africans in a language which, Beth informed me, was known as Kitchen Bember, a dialect commonly used throughout Southern Africa by mining communities. Every other sentence seemed to consist of lappa this or lappa that, which perhaps explains why the Northern Territories were often referred to as Lappa-Lappa-Land! Occasionally Ian would send the children outside with Cokes for the labourers, who worked up quite a thirst digging out the foundations in the scorching heat of an October sun.

Karl and Craig would sometimes join us for a cup of tea on the stoep. While Craig, lost in thought, hardly uttered a word, Karl would chat away enthusiastically, discussing various aspects concerning the job in hand. Although I tried to take an interest in the proceedings, more often than not I found these sessions to be too technical and was often blinded by science.

The pool turned out to be kidney-shaped, and measured approximately sixteen square feet. Inside it sloped gradually from a shallow metre to over seven at the deep end. One day a large piece of machinery appeared in what was left of the front garden. Driven at speed, it sprayed gallons of cement over the wire netting base which now covered the inside of the pool. Once solid, the concrete surface was plastered carefully to a smooth finish and then left for a couple of days to dry out completely.

It was at this crucial stage of the proceedings that our neighbours' Alsatian, Skipper, decided to investigate under the cover of darkness. Much to the annoyance of all concerned, he left a trail of paw prints in the wet cement for posterity. Eventually rows of multicoloured mosaic tiles were neatly arranged around the sides and steps of the pool.

Using a couple of garden hosepipes it took two to three days to fill the pool with water. Although the local fire brigade could have completed the job in a couple of hours, we were warned that the water they supplied was often polluted.

I soon became aware that there were less attractive aspects to owning a pool. Maintaining a constant supply of chlorine, pool acid and various spare parts at a time when import licences were hard to come by, proved to be a marathon task. But one soon learnt to improvise.

Once the flagstones surrounding the pool had been laid, the garden boy repaired what was left of the damaged front lawn. As grass seed was unobtainable locally, I watched him painstakingly transfer numerous blades of grass from other parts of the garden. Some twelve months later I was astounded by the lush green lawn, which was much in evidence.

We all lost complete control one afternoon, towards the end of November, when Karl appeared on the scene, announcing those magical words, 'The pool's all yours, man.' Everyone greeted this statement by yelling ecstatically 'Lekker man!' – an expression Karl used constantly when something pleased him.

5

Karl Theron was a keen and knowledgeable gardener. It was due to him and a close friend of his who owned Kalemba Nurseries, that our pool terrace and surrounding garden took on such colourful splendour.

Once the pool had been completed a high stone wall was erected, painted white to accentuate the green of the lawns and foliage. A dotted path of slabs led to the wire safety fence around the pool area, which in time became smothered in summer's bougainvillaea, with a hint of autumn's azaleas. Various shrubs and bushes, too numerous to mention, soon grew in abundance.

A row of Pride of India trees stood spanning the drive, their pink and white blossoms seasonally strewn and abandoned like pieces of confetti. Clumps of frangipani, with splashes of pink and creamy white flowering clusters, graced the far corners. Whenever possible I would sit awhile to indulge in the sheer beauty of it all.

Once the pool had been completed Karl continued to visit us from time to time. Anthony and Fiona were always delighted to see him. This was due, mainly, to the fact that upon his departure he would give them a ride in the back of this pick-up to the far end of the crescent. Ian would then time the children as they raced back home across the green in front of the bungalow. Although it was a foregone conclusion who would be the winner, Fiona never failed to compete relentlessly.

I first met Karl's daughter, Celeste, one evening after having invited them over to dine with us. At the time, Karl's wife, Ivy, was visiting relatives overseas. When I asked them how they were managing on their own both father and daughter claimed to be coping adequately with the help of the houseboy, who was well trained and reliable. They admitted, however, that planning and preparing meals was becoming something of a chore, which they took in turns. It appeared Ivy had never found it necessary to employ a chef, preferring to manage the cooking entirely on her own.

Karl then stated with pride, 'When it comes to catering my wife is nothing less than a connoisseur.'

'Presumably the houseboy does most of the clearing up, then,' I queried, feeling somewhat disgruntled. In reply he looked to his daughter for support. However, Celeste's immediate reaction was that she had not the foggiest idea as, unlike her mother, she loathed all forms of domesticity. 'Someone with a kindred spirit,' I reflected appreciatively.

No effort had been spared on my part when planning and preparing the meal that evening. To state that I had gone to a great deal of trouble would have been an understatement. Consequently, I was mortified to discover that the homemade mushroom soup had developed lumps when my back was turned. Without success, I searched desperately for the sieve I had seen lying in the Wendy house some days earlier. How I wished I had retrieved it at the time. Groaning inwardly, I offered up a silent prayer as I grabbed the tea strainer from the draining board. For what appeared to be an eternity, I forced most of the lumpy liquid through what seemed to be microscopic holes.

Thankfully, my prayers were answered, for when the meal finally materialised my guests gave not the slightest hint that they found anything to be less than perfect, and appeared to have excellent appetites. Upon reflection, I must admit that due to the unavoidable delay a more than generous amount of 'aperitif' had been consumed beforehand. Taking a leaf out of Ivy's book, I left the clearing away for the houseboy, making a mental note to establish an all out effort to find a reliable cookboy.

We found Celeste to be an attractive teenager with a sunny disposition. She kept us entertained by relating various amusing incidents from the past, in which she and her friends had participated. Not one word, however, was mentioned about her most up-to-date escapade. Outraged, Karl had confided recently that he had been obliged to pay a flying visit to Johannesburg to extract his daughter from the clutches of a married man. I got the definite impression, however, that the chief cause of his displeasure was the fact that the gentleman in question once had designs on Celeste's mother!

That evening there was no apparent evidence that Celeste was suffering from a broken heart. On the contrary, she chatted away cheerfully about life in general. At one point, however, she mentioned philosophically that she had returned to the Copperbelt in order to sort out her life and plan for the future.

As fate had it, she did neither. Some time later I learnt that she had fallen desperately in love with Nicco, a handsome Asian youth whom she had known since childhood. When the relationship ended abruptly with Celeste packing her bags and returning to Johannesburg, although Karl was adamant that he had not been the instigator, I was convinced he had played no small part in dissolving the partnership.

After dinner we did not return to the stoep as the evening had turned chilly. Instead we sipped our coffee in the front room with the stereo playing softly in the background. Although at first reluctant, prompted by his daughter, Karl entertained us with snippets from his past.

Leaving university footloose and fancy free, apart from a diploma in agriculture, he possessed little of any value with which to face the future. With the eagerness of youth he turned his hand to various enterprising ventures, none of which proved to be successful. At one stage he took to sea, working on a whaler. We listened enthralled to his seafaring adventures, when life was arduous and conditions squalid. Returning to Port Elizabeth after his final voyage, he felt compelled to destroy most of his clothing and personal belongings in order to rid himself of the appalling stench of fish which engulfed everything.

Turning his back on South Africa, he decided to seek his fortunes elsewhere. Nearly penniless, he arrived in Northern Rhodesia – renamed Zambia since Independence. It did not take him long to realise that farming was a viable proposition. Before he was able to put this to the test, in order to survive he signed on as a general assistant with a copper mining company. What had started out as a temporary measure, however, became a permanent position when he was offered promotion a few months later. Inheriting most of the problems along with this achievement, he sometimes wondered if he had made a wise decision when finally abandoning his dreams of becoming a farmer.

In those days, Ivy sang with a group called The Flamboyants. They performed regularly at a local nightspot where they were extremely popular, attracting large audiences. Karl, a regular visitor, soon became infatuated with the delectable vocalist. At first she ignored his advances, but eventually yielded to his wit and charm.

On their first date Karl thought Ivy looked sensational and informed her that she looked like a million dollars. 'Thanks a bundle but for your information you're not getting a single cent,' was her spontaneous reply.

'How wrong she was,' Karl contemplated, adding triumphantly, 'I won the jackpot, for we were married the following Christmas.'

Turning to Celeste he put his arm around her shoulder, stating affectionately, 'Celeste arrived as a Christmas present, twelve months later.'

As the years rolled by and the pressure of work increased, Karl found his position with the mines becoming less and less rewarding. Shortly after Independence he was introduced to a fellow Dutchman who had recently purchased a small cement business. It materialised that the man was short of capital and was considering taking on a partner. This seemed to be a heavensent opportunity which Karl, without further ado, grasped with both hands.

At the time the house they were living in was owned by the mining company. Consequently, upon his resignation, he had to start looking for somewhere else to live. Nearly all his savings had gone into the new venture; hence previous plans for the new house he had contemplated building across the river had to be put on hold. In the meantime he rented a small property from a family who had gone overseas on long leave.

Many months of hard work and continually living on a shoestring began to pay off as the company slowly became solvent. From that point onwards any spare time and money went into completing their dream home. It was with a sense of accomplishment that Karl and Ivy moved across the river when the bungalow was finally ready for occupation. Originally of extremely modest proportions, over the years the property was extended in line with the family's needs and company's profits.

Karl concluded by remarking that having finally cultivated some of the surrounding hectares, which were now yielding quite a handsome profit, he had proved that his degree in agriculture had not been a complete waste of time.

As our guests made to leave, thanking us for our hospitality, Karl mentioned that he particularly appreciated all the effort I had gone to on their account. I couldn't help but blush, as I replied nonchalantly, 'Not at all, it was merely a question of setting a couple of extra places!'

6

Shortly after Ivy returned from overseas we received an invitation to spend Sunday on Karl's farm across the river. I must admit, from his flowing description, I had certain reservations about meeting his wife, who I fancied to be a combination of Ava Gardner and Wonder Woman. As I got to know her better, however, she turned out to be quite normal; not quite the paragon of virtue that I had once imagined her to be.

To reach the farm was a venture in itself. Entering Mine Town, we drove to the bottom of Central Street, nicknamed Sesame Street by the children for reasons best known to themselves. We forked left just below the police station, where a dirt road led us through a thick forest for about a kilometre. Upon reaching the Kafue River, we were brought to an abrupt halt by a large brick building which housed several cars. Ian parked in a sheltered spot under some trees before going to investigate further.

The children spotted a signpost which bore the inscription 'Gekkehuis' which, when loosely translated, means bedlam. Presumably this inscription referred to times long gone, bearing little resemblance to the Therons' present, organised lifestyle. Below the sign was a large red button with the instruction 'Druk'. Ignoring Anthony's pleas, Ian lifted Fiona so that she could press the button, while I attempted to pacify our son with the promise that it would be his turn next time.

Anthony's disappointed protests died away as a persistent whirring sound stole his attention. Silently we watched as within minutes a sturdy steel cage, travelling along overhead cables, came into view. As it came to a sudden halt above a flight of steep, wooden steps the excited children clambered up, followed more cautiously by Ian and me.

The embankment fell away as the tightly packed cage once again swung into action. Filled with a sudden spirit of adventure, we gazed

29

around in delight at the panoramic view of river and countryside. Although our eyes eagerly scanned both banks for any sign of wildlife, we saw nothing of great interest. Soaring high above the treacherous flow, we were blissfully unaware of those times when we would barely skim the surface of the murky, crocodile-infested river.

Reaching the far bank, the cage came to a smooth halt. As we alighted Karl was waiting to welcome us. Turning our backs on the Kafue, we followed him up a sharp incline leading into woodland. Pausing briefly, he pointed to a complicated piece of machinery whose function, he explained, was to generate enough electricity to supply the needs of the farmhouse, as well as operate the cage. Interrupting our murmurs of admiration, he revealed that the system had its drawbacks, which included the occasional breakdown. 'Consequently,' he admitted ruefully, 'anyone unfortunate enough to be travelling across the river by cage is left stranded until the supply is restored.'

As we weaved our way through a narrow grassy dell bordering the surrounding thicket, our host proceeded to relate how his own wife had once been an unsuspecting victim during a horrendous thunderstorm. Marooned for over two hours, dangling only a few inches above the swiftly flowing water, she had suffered a panic attack while waiting to be rescued. 'Rather than risk a repeat performance, during the rainy season she now drives into town taking the old dirt track, crossing the Kafue bridge north of Kwatcha Compound,' Karl concluded.

We soon reached a small wrought iron gate through which, in the distance, we spotted a lady in a kneeling position. Dressed in a white sundress and matching wide-brimmed hat, she arose as we approached, carefully adjusting her skirt. Waving, she called out, 'I'm just finishing a spot of pruning.' In evidence, a pile of rose cuttings and a pair of secateurs lay discarded on the lawn. While Karl did the necessary introductions, there was no denying that his wife, whilst no longer in her first flush of youth, was extremely elegant and attractive.

With the promise of a refreshing glass of home-made lemonade, Ivy led us towards the bungalow, which was fronted by a large, comfortably furnished stoep. Karl mentioned that they had bought the wicker furniture from the local ecumenical centre, run by missionary priests. Following on where her husband had left off, Ivy expounded that everything on sale at the centre was handmade by local handicapped people, the majority of whom were blind. 'To help fund this enterprise,' she continued, 'a number of volunteers have set up a small shop in the grounds, where items, ranging from homegrown produce to exotically embroidered caftans, can be purchased at realistic prices.' At her suggestion, I readily agreed to accompany her on her next visit to the centre.

A low brick wall, smothered in Virginia creeper, encompassed the stoep. Mosaic-clad steps reached the matching floor, most of which was covered by rush matting. Suspended from the ceiling, earthenware pots failed to restrain leafy trailers which clung for support to eye-catching, macrame-knotted strands of fibre. The overall effect supplemented an atmosphere of tranquillity.

Tea, served on the stoep, consisted of scrumptious home-baked scones filled with lashings of strawberry jam and clotted cream. An enormous chocolate gateau proved too much of a temptation for all of us. When the tea trolley was once more confined to the kitchen, Ivy suggested a short tour of inspection. Needing no second bidding, I eagerly followed our hostess through a pair of French windows.

At the end of a narrow anteroom we entered a spacious, elegantly furnished, sitting room. The mahogany parquet floor was partially concealed by two rectangular Persian rugs. In between stood a large stinkwood table, its centre graced by a magnificent lead crystal rose bowl. Suspended above was a matching chandelier – shimmering soft rainbows of light as the late afternoon sun caught its attention. Scattered around the room, several pieces of old Dutch marquetry added to the overall grandeur, reflected in a full-sized mirror.

A handsome stone fireplace, displaying a sparkling array of brasswork, spanned the far wall. From a lofty position above the chimney breast the portrait of a Spanish dancer surveyed the scene. A decorative comb, adorning thick black tresses, surrounded a delicately defined face, which wore a rather doleful expression.

Karl told us that they had bought the painting at an auction some years ago because it bore such a striking resemblance to his wife. This no one could dispute. Furthermore, in time I was to witness a similar wistful expression appear on Ivy's face when she felt she had been thwarted. Whether this was due to coincidence or hours of patient practice could be anybody's guess!

Taking into account the opulence of the sitting room, by comparison the rest of the house appeared unpretentious. In all fairness it was an established fact that quality imports were considered to be luxuries of a bygone age.

Leaving the house we were guided towards a large brick construction without windows. This turned out to be a squash court. According to Ivy, Karl having planned it, then built it, now spent every spare moment within its confines. 'Most evenings I'm lucky to catch a glimpse of him before supper time,' she protested.

When Karl challenged Ian to a game of squash the fact that he had arrived completely unprepared proved to be of little consequence. Hanging in a cupboard in the changing room was a generous selection of sports attire, along with numerous pairs of plimsolls, referred to as takkies.

It came as no surprise when Ivy admitted that squash was not one of her favourite pastimes. Suggesting I stay behind and watch the men play for a while, she volunteered to look after the children who had disappeared in the direction of the swimming pool. 'I can keep an eye on them while I prepare the braai near the pool area. Join me there when you've had enough,' was her parting shot.

I made my way up to a large balcony from where I was able to get an all over view of the court. It became abundantly obvious that, in this location, no expense had been spared. Resting my elbows on the guard rail, I gazed down and let my gaze travel steadily across well-seasoned floor boards. Inching their way up lofty white walls divided by a symmetrical guideline, my eyes finally came to rest upon the ceiling. With the flick of a switch, carefully protected fluorescent tubes highlighted a pair of extractor fans built into the structure.

Once the contest was in progress, although Ian was no novice, it soon became apparent that those hours his opponent had spent before supper each evening had been put to good purpose – Karl won hands down.

While the two men changed, from the comfort of a large armchair I once more concentrated on my surroundings. Facing me, at the back of the balcony, was a horseshoe bar on whose polished surface stood a replica of a canon. The mahogany base was designed to hold a bottle of cognac; once in place the funnel-shaped neck formed the gun barrel. Behind the bar a tray of tumblers and goblets had been placed on what later proved to be a well-stocked refrigerator.

When Ian and Karl came upstairs to quench their thirst, before joining them, I decided to inspect the scene below. Steep stairs, leading from the balcony, paused opposite a small opening to the squash court, before descending to the changing room. Inside, thick towelling robes, hanging from strategically placed hooks close to the shower, waited invitingly to be wrapped around dripping shoulders. An assortment of irresistible lotions and powders beckoned from the top of a pine cabinet, tempting me to stop and sample their contents.

We eventually emerged revitalised and made for the pool area. The children rushed to meet us, waving thick wedges of the gateau left over from teatime. Between mouthfuls they proceeded to give us a detailed account of how they had helped to build the braai.

For our benefit they then insisted upon demonstrating their newly perfected art of manufacturing paper spills. Clutching several large sheets of newspaper, they rolled each one into a tube which they flattened before plaiting. They explained that the spills went at the very bottom of the braai before being covered by dry twigs, which in turn were covered with handfuls of charcoal. To their utter delight, at this stage, the garden boy had doused the whole thing in petrol before igniting it with a lighted match. 'The flames leapt right into the air and so did Auntie Ivy,' they revealed gleefully.

If somewhat dangerous, this method certainly was to prove most effective when we put it to the test at a later date. Another useful tip we picked up that evening was that a little beer used to dampen down the flames improved the flavour of the food decidedly.

The Therons had invited a few close friends around to join them for the braai that evening. Whilst waiting for everyone to arrive we sipped glasses of chilled wine, trying to ignore the tantalising aroma drifting towards us.

When all the guests had arrived we were invited to help ourselves to succulent steaks, halves of chicken and the inevitable boerwors. Jacket potatoes, cooked in foil, dripping in butter and cheese, beckoned compellingly from the edge of the grill.

That night, as the dying embers lost their glow, it soon became evident that the time for more serious drinking was rapidly approaching. After a couple of quickies for the road, we gathered up the children who were already half asleep. Before making tracks for home we thanked our hosts for what could only have been described as an absolutely perfect day.

7

The Zambian climate can be divided roughly into three periods. The hot dry summer season puts in a tranquil appearance around the end of August, lifting everybody's spirit. During October, re-christened Suicide Month, the temperature soars, leaving one feeling drained; praying for the rains to arrive. These can develop, any time from mid-October onwards, accompanied by their own particular trials and tribulations. With the sudden demise of the rainy season around the end of April, a certain chill in the air heralds the arrival of winter to complete the annual cycle.

Winter brought hours of glorious sunshine and blue skies, as cooling winds dispersed any rain clouds which might still be gathering. When the sun refused to shine temperatures plummeted. On chilly evenings we would sit snugly in front of a huge log fire, reminiscent of Christmas card scenes of a bygone era.

From the middle of June all but the most stalwart amongst us found the water to be far too cold for either lessons or relaxation, the keen biting wind compelling us to keep our shoulders well under the water.

Ground frost, although uncommon, was not unheard of during the months of June and July. An unseasonable short sharp shower was also known to put in the occasional appearance during August.

One winter I joined a group of housewives who were learning how to ice cakes for special occasions. Sofia ran the class, proving to be an excellent teacher. Although no effort was spared on my part, the finished results were often less than perfect. After much practice, however, I eventually achieved what I had begun to think was the impossible, and was even approached by a friend to decorate a cake for her wedding anniversary!

At Ian's suggestion, another time I sent away for a foreign language course. Once the books and tapes arrived, full of good intentions, I settled down to improve my knowledge of the French language. Sadly, however, on this occasion, I made very little progress.

As the chilly winds of winter receded, it became apparent that summer, a time to return to the outdoor life, was fast approaching. Aquatic distractions once more became the order of the day, as winter pastimes were provisionally dismissed. Boatyards and slipways were invaded by enthusiasts dedicated to restoring recently neglected motor, rowing and sailing craft. With drill and paintbrush at the ready, each proud owner worked with vigour, eager to be off and away on the enticing water.

Braai drums and grills were scrubbed till they shone. Picnic hampers, along with water skies and wet suits, were all given a thorough airing. Any spare space in the freezer was allocated for braai packs while fridges were re-stocked with wine and beer and Jolly juice.

Early summer was indeed an idyllic season; a time for people of all ages to enjoy life, with one momentous day following another. The highlight of the season was the commodore's ball. Although the occasion was held in and around the clubhouse it was a formal affair when the gentlemen wore dinner jackets and were accompanied by ladies dressed in lavish ball gowns. To be invited to sit at the commodore's table was a great privilege, extended only to those who had proved themselves noteworthy during regattas and the like over the past twelve months.

As the summer came to a climax I dreaded those sultry stifling days when the sun was almost obscured by the dust-clogged environment. Although a heavy downpour was responsible for helping to clear the atmosphere I, nevertheless, found it extremely difficult to come to terms with the sticky, humid, rainy season. John, our houseboy, each year would forecast that the rains should arrive on the 15th November. He wasn't far out either for, with a certain regularity, the first heavy shower usually occurred around this date.

Although we had experienced the odd false alarm during the month of November, we were to experience a late start to the rainy season during our first year in Zambia. As far as I was concerned, this proved to be a bonus as I was able to continue giving swimming lessons, undisturbed by thunderstorms.

Christmas had been and gone, before masses of dark threatening clouds rolled across the cobalt sky, heralding the arrival of the rains in earnest. I was shortly to learn, to my dismay, that a continuous downpour, accompanied by lightning, could be responsible for my having to cancel a whole day's swimming schedule. Due to atmospherics, the telephone was always out of order, making it impossible for me to contact pupils in order to make alternative arrangements at short notice.

Each horrendous storm took on a similar pattern. Intensifying flashes of light acted as a beacon in the sky which became resonant with the sound of approaching thunder. Without warning, jagged forks of lightning attacked the copper-laden earth with unrelenting ferocity. The first gentle drops of rain intensified, cascading down on the corrugated roofs of houses, almost deafening the inhabitants. Storm drains overflowed as the persistent torrent turned roads into rivers, leaving gardens looking like paddy fields. The surrounding shanty towns were especially vulnerable. Bent upon destroying all but the sturdiest of structures in its wake the storm left a trail of desolation and despair everywhere, before abating as abruptly as it began.

No longer menacing, each exhausted cloud shed its silver lining, which for a while filtered away the sticky, stifling humidity, leaving everything refreshed and revitalised. Little pools of water, left behind in evidence, soon evaporated as the prevalent sun reappeared and stroked the saturated earth with its strong warm fingers.

Flushed out of various nooks and crannies by untold summer storms, numerous insects invaded the privacy of every home without exception. Spider-shaped ticks found refuge in skirting boards where they lay in wait to tap the life-giving blood of unsuspecting victims. Putzi flies gathered in profusion round lines full of washing, ready to lay their eggs on the soft damp fibre. Once dry, every article had to be pressed with a cotton hot iron to decimate each microscopic egg concealed within numerous seams and folds.

One year I discovered, to my cost, that simply sitting on a damp towel, left to dry by the side of the pool, could result in misery. When the housegirl next door confirmed that the massive irritating lump on my right thigh undoubtedly housed a putzi grub, I felt invaded.

Taking her advice, I smothered the inflamed swelling generously in Vaseline jelly before covering it with an airtight plaster. A few days later, mustering up all my willpower, I gingerly squeezed the throbbing abscess, in order to remove the perpetrator. To my disgust, it had grown into a greyish-coloured maggot measuring approximately half an inch in length! Although the physical wound soon disappeared, it was quite some time before the psychological scar was healed.

The dogs had to be deloused regularly. If their wounds were left to fester they could develop tick fever, the outcome of which often proved fatal. Normally John volunteered to carry out the gruesome task of removing both maggots and bloated ticks, embedded in the animals' thick fur.

Snakes of every shape and description appeared in and around the pool and garden. Few of them proved to be dangerous and those that were, fortunately, being of a timid nature, usually preferred to keep well out of harm's way. The spitting cobra, however, was something to be reckoned with. John cornered one in a drain, one afternoon, shortly after a heavy downpour. We pointed it out to Ian when he returned home from work. As Ian peered down the drain in order to get a closer look, the incensed reptile spat into his face. Fortunately, my husband was wearing a pair of sunglasses at the time, which prevented the venomous liquid from blinding him. Needless to say he made short work of the snake.

Although the very thought of it now fills me with shame, through ignorance we would kill quite harmless reptiles indiscriminately. On one occasion, with the help of a golf club, I bludgeoned to death a small cobra which had taken refuge in my neighbour's bathroom. Afterwards, we both teased the security guard who had, from a safe distance, brandished his baton, yelling words of encouragement!

Eventually I learnt the error of my ways from a wildlife enthusiast who, with the aid of a fairly long stick, demonstrated how, with a little patience and dexterity, the most stubborn trespasser could be persuaded to return to its own domain. My mentor proved to be so skilful that afterwards I wondered if he could possibly have practised on vipers of the human variety.

I failed dismally, however, to put his theory to the test on one such occasion, just after we had moved to Solweizi Avenue. At the time, feeling disinclined to join Ian and the children, who were glued to the television watching a football match, for a while I wandered around aimlessly. After what seemed like an eternity, thinking that the match must be over, I returned to the front room only to be met by the words 'extra time'. Groaning inwardly, I decided to console myself with a glass of wine normally kept for special occasions. It was a balmy evening and before long I felt completely at ease with the world as I relaxed on the patio. Suddenly my eyes rested on a dividing wall a few yards away, painted a dismal shade of green. Making a mental note to have it painted white at the end of the rainy season, I meandered over to inspect the colourful creeper which concealed part of the eyesore. Hungrily I savoured the tantalizing aroma from a neighbouring braai which wafted over the garden wall.

Suddenly, a strange sensation transferred my attention from my stomach to my right foot, as I felt something sliding across it. Glancing down curiously, I was horrified to discover a snake encircling my ankle. Instinctively, using all the strength I could muster, I jerked my foot upwards, in order to dislodge the reptile. It was with a great sense of relief that I watched the snake catapult through the air before landing under a tree some distance away. Once more in control, I approached my assailant with great caution, to discover that it had been rendered senseless.

Rushing back into the house I started to relate my disturbing experience to what I imagined would be a sympathetic ear. Contrary to all expectation, however, the only response I received was 'Quiet!' This was immediately followed by, 'It's a goal – Yeeeees!' Somewhat crestfallen, I left the victorious fans to their moment of glory and returned to the seclusion of the patio and the still prostrate viper.

8

Once the pool was fully functional, I decided to occupy my afternoons teaching swimming; something I had always enjoyed doing. When I mentioned the idea to Karl he was most enthusiastic and promised to pass the word around.

My first pupils were three little girls from the mine school, who soon persuaded several of their friends to join them. I charged a modest fee for my efforts, having learnt from bitter experience that, generally, most people only seem to appreciate what they pay for.

Around that time I paid a visit to Parklands to inquire if I could advertise my services in one of the stores in the precinct. From a distance, I spotted a plate glass window plastered in what appeared to be advertisements. On close inspection, however, I was somewhat taken aback to discover that each neatly typed card bore details of patrons who had neglected to pay their bills on time.

Curiosity soon got the better of me and as I glanced at the list of debtors it became apparent that not all of them were of limited means. Pinned centrally, between a Mr P.J. Singh and Miss Grace Banda, was an entry bearing the prodigious title 'Mrs R.B. Fortescue-Jones,' a person of some standing in the community!

Abandoning my mission, I retraced my steps, deciding that it would be simpler to increase my roll by word of mouth. I had considered advertising in a local newspaper but thought better of it as, at the time, I had not yet applied for a work permit. As it turned out, thanks to the grapevine I soon had enough students, including adults, to keep me occupied most mornings and afternoons.

At the end of the first month I could think of no pleasanter way of spending my earnings than by having an informal get-together. Ian, naturally, thought this was a splendid idea, so we decided to invite most of our friends to a lunchtime braai. We realised we were taking a risk holding it in the open a few weeks into the rainy season but this did not dampen our ardour in the slightest. As the great day approached, however, I silently prayed that the occasion would not be spoilt by a sudden downpour.

Not being used to catering for more than a handful of people, I was at first more than a trifle apprehensive, wondering whether or not I should be able to cope on my own. By a stroke of luck, however, I was introduced to Amy, whose husband was on a short term contract with the Power Corporation. We soon became the best of friends and like a good Samaritan she volunteered her services for the occasion, producing a variety of attractive salads and side dishes.

My next door neighbour, Donna, also came to my aid, spending hours creating all kinds of mouthwatering delights. These she slipped surreptitiously across the dividing garden wall. Sworn to secrecy, both friends were fully aware that I would unashamedly take full credit for their efforts. I cannot begin to express how much I missed Amy and Donna when their husbands' contracts expired within a few weeks of one another and they returned to live in England the following summer.

Charles Lang assured me that he knew a farmer who supplied the most mouthwatering braai packs, containing boerwors prepared from a well guarded recipe. 'Just leave that side of things to me,' he volunteered, before explaining in detail how these long coils of sausage were prepared.

'To be concise', he pontificated, 'coriander, nutmeg and cloves are added to proportionate amounts of beef, mutton and pork. Various herbs and spices are added to the ingredients which are then put through the mincer. Finally the mixture is squeezed into one long sausage skin measuring several feet in length. This can be cooked either whole or, if preferred, cut into small portions beforehand.' As an afterthought he then confided, 'A braai without boerwors, my dear, can well be compared to a pub without beer!'

For his part, Ian organised the drinks and hired a massive cooler from the Copper Belt Bottling Company. I did all the necessary panicking and the children got into everyone's way, quite convinced they were indispensable.

In spite of my qualms, on the day in question everything seemed to go according to plan. The weather was perfect without even the hint of a shower. The only cloud on the horizon turned out to be that although the meat and wors proved to be every bit as excellent as

41

Charles had predicted, he had skimped on the order, which resulted in meagre second helpings.

The occasion cannot be dismissed completely without mentioning one small incident, involving David Roberts and his wife, Caroline.

It was a well-known fact that Mrs Roberts absolutely refused to sacrifice her life in suburbia for the wilds of Africa. However, she occasionally accompanied the three children when they visited their father during the summer holidays. That year, however, quite out of keeping, she made a surprise visit which caused quite a stir. When David relayed our invitation to the braai to his wife, she accepted without a quibble. As it transpired, she seemed to know several of the other guests present, which, as it happened, turned out to be a blessing in disguise.

Due to the celibate lifestyle David claimed to lead, it was hardly surprising that he had an eye for every pretty girl in sight. Where other men check first before enjoying the discreet glance or occasional eyeful, David was known to throw all caution to the wind. The day of our party proved to be no exception. At first, I noticed he was extremely attentive towards his wife, fetching and carrying drinks for her and her companions, with cigarettes and lighter ever at the ready.

Caroline, fortunately, chose to mingle well away from the pool area, content to recline on the stoep with several slightly more mature couples. From their attire, it was apparent that not one of them had the slightest intention of taking part in any aquatic activity. They appeared to be engrossed in a conversation which was, presumably, both entertaining and amusing judging from the general air of cheerfulness which prevailed.

When David eventually managed to escape, he ensconced himself in a chair by the pool side, where he seemed to be in his element. One by one, he examined each bikini-clad female in turn, before focusing his complete attention upon Amy.

After lunch the majority of our guests idled the time away chatting over cups of coffee, or something stronger. David seemed content to relax on his own and ogle Amy who was cooling off in the pool. Not wishing to draw attention to his well-nourished body, he had remained fully clothed, shielding his rather ruddy complexion with a large pair of sunglasses and wide-brimmed bush hat. The only time

42

he relinquished his vantage point overlooking the pool was when he got up to replenish his empty glass. He had just returned to his seat after one such quest, when the following incident took everyone by surprise.

Caroline, having weighed up the situation, advanced stealthily towards the pool area, waiting for the right moment to come along. Completely oblivious, David moved to the edge of the pool, in order to assist Amy from the water. Grabbing the opportunity with both hands, Caroline went into action, lunging at her husband's posterior as he, unwittingly, lent forward. Teetering on the brink for a fraction of a second in a frantic effort to steady himself, he then executed a perfect belly-flop on top of poor Amy.

The children behaved as if the whole thing had been staged especially for their benefit, much to the delight of the majority of onlookers. Ian eventually succeeded in freeing the bewildered David from the clutches of a cheering, yelling mob of juveniles. After several attempts someone managed to retrieve his false teeth from the bottom of the pool. Fortunately, they appeared to be none the worse for the ducking, which is more than can be said for our guest.

Much to their credit, if either of the Roberts bore any ill-feeling towards their partner, they kept it to themselves, behaving as if the whole incident had been a huge joke. Furthermore, Amy and her husband accepted the whole affair with equal good humour. For this Ian and I were more than grateful. After all, what could have proved to be a disastrous situation, instead turned out to be an amusing talking point with which to entertain family and friends for some time to come.

9

'Fancy a visit to the Victoria Falls?' Ian enquired nonchalantly one evening.

'Yeees!' the children and I sang out in unison, unable to contain our excitement. For the next ten minutes, all bedlam was let loose as Anthony, Fiona and I bombarded him with questions.

We had been living in Zambia for about six months and during this period a visit to Livingstone had been at the top of our list of priorities. We were well aware, however, that if we waited until the end of the rainy season the Zambezi would be in full flood, resulting in clouds of spray obscuring magnificent views of the gorge. Summer's long dry spell, on the other hand, would reduce the flow to a slow trickle.

'I've arranged to take some time off at the beginning of January,' Ian announced, when he was able to get a word in edgeways. He went on to explain that as the rains had arrived much later than expected that year, it should be an ideal time for a visit. 'I'm putting out feelers to see if there is a chance we can spend a few days in Rhodesia when we leave Livingstone, but don't set your hopes too high,' he added as an afterthought.

For the next couple of months Ian planned the trip meticulously. As the border post at Livingstone was closed it meant we would have to cross the Zambezi at Kazangula, forty miles up river, and enter Rhodesia from Botswana. There seemed to be no end of red tape to be dealt with beforehand. This included applying for a current tax clearance certificate and permit to take the car abroad. Proof that the four of us had recently been immunised against yellow fever and cholera was another requisite. It seemed incredible that one had to go to such lengths in order to view the Falls from the opposite bank of the river.

We knew of no one who had made the journey recently, so Ian had to do all the spade work. Not that this deterred him in the slightest, being of the opinion that nothing ventured is nothing gained.

Tingling with excitement, we set off before dawn one morning towards the end of January. Skirting the centre of Kitwe, we drove through deserted streets, making for the Ndola Road. Once my eyes had grown accustomed to the surrounding darkness, I searched the horizon in the hope of seeing tippings being discarded from the local copper mine. At last my efforts were rewarded as a carpet of red hot embers rolled over the edge of the man-made mountain ahead; a most spectacular sight.

For several miles past the Luanshya bypass we were entertained by night owls resting on the tarmac. As the car approached them at considerable speed we held our breath in consternation. Perched in the centre of the road, eyes glinting defiantly in the headlights, they seemed to wait until the very last moment before spreading their wings for take-off.

Quite suddenly the night sky lightened, causing mysterious shapes and objects to stand out starkly against the rapidly expanding rose-tinted horizon. Our silent world sprang to life as a multitude of birds tuned into nature, broadcasting far and wide.

At the start of a new day local villagers, relying upon nature's rays to light their path, trundled out of the surrounding bush. Mothers with babies attached to their backs were followed closely by toddlers and school-aged children protesting sleepily as they made for the nearest township.

Our first port of call was Kapiri Mposhi, one of several bustling townships which had sprung up along the line of rail. On the outskirts we stopped to watch a steam engine being shunted onto a gigantic turntable, which then rotated slowly.

Taking the advice of friends, we stopped for a delicious English breakfast at a small café nearby. As the toilet facilities were out of action we were directed to the one and only hotel, named the Village Pump. I imagined sentimentally that it must have been built on the site of some old well or watering hole. As we left, however, Ian commented dryly that the Village Dump would have been a more appropriate title, thus dispelling any romantic notions on my part. Unfortunately, he had snagged his trousers on a nail in the men's washroom and was not in the best of moods.

All was forgotten, however, by the time we reached Kabwe, once known as Broken Hill, renowed for its silver and copper mines.

Driving past endless rows of dilapidated shops and houses I found it difficult to imagine there had been a time when Kabwe was a hive of industry and social activities.

We soon flashed past Landless Corner. This well-known milestone, surrounded by hectares of arable land, was once nothing but a wilderness. Now something of an oasis, it had been cultivated by British settlers around the turn of the century.

Joining the bottleneck of traffic streaming into Lusaka, we cruised at a less then leisurely pace, viewing what appeared to be a decaying capital. A number of recently built tower blocks failed dismally to compensate for the overall picture of neglect.

Just past the football stadium a banner spanned the highway, proclaiming that Zambia was enjoying her tenth year of independence. Further on we took the opportunity to examine a monument erected to celebrate the end of colonialism. Depicting the figure of a man, back bent, breaking loose from chains of bondage, it inspired much speculation.

Deciding to break our journey, we stopped at the Ridgeway for refreshments. Entering the hotel, we stepped into a different world entirely. The elegant interior hinted at an era long gone. Through a pair of French windows we made our way to the verandah which overlooked a well-stocked pond. Here we enjoyed glasses of ice-cold lemonade, while watching rainbow-tinted fish dart in and out of their rocky terrain. Straddling the pond a carved wooden bridge led to the dining room, where tables draped in spotless linen displayed glittering crystal surrounded by silver. Though tempted we did not stay for lunch, or fritter our time away in the enticing swimming pool, open to non-residents.

Once we had left the bustling streets of the capital, the road to Mazabuka stretched endlessly in front of us. On the way we passed several interesting landmarks, including an open-air cinema known as the Bio. Our favourite, however, was the witch doctor's sign set up in opposition to the old mission church a few yards further on.

The further south we travelled damboes and scrubland gave way to rolling hills; once elephant country. Far off, growing in the wilderness, the odd flamboyant tree added a splash of crimson to the sombre landscape. In comparison, the drab old baobab flourished in

46

clumps with dreary, almost leafless branches and thick distorted trunks entwined grotesquely.

According to mythology, long before the white man ever set foot on the continent, this much admired tree suffered a terrible affliction. One fateful day, for some unknown reason, its presence provoked the wrath of the devil who, in a fury, tore through the land uprooting every baobab in sight. Completely exhausted the demon then fell asleep for several days. When he awoke refreshed, seeing the havoc he had caused, he regretted his impulsive behaviour. Retracing his steps, he attempted to repair much of the damage. It soon became apparent, however, that those trees still alive were wilting rapidly. Compelled to complete the task in great haste, the devil planted many of them upside down.

As we journeyed south, the atmosphere became increasingly humid. Threatening storm clouds gathered overhead, obliterating any sign of the sun. As we drove past acres of sugar cane on the out-skirts of Mazabuka, an ear-splitting crash of thunder signalled the start of a horrendous hailstorm. Visibility became poor and driving proved to be a nerve-racking experience. To add to our discomfort, without warning, we suddenly ran out of tarmac. We were then com-pelled to drive along a dirt track for several miles.

Some of our worst moments were when the car skidded and slid sideways over the slimy surface. During this period, we were sub-jected to a deafening din as gigantic hailstones pounded the roof of the car. As we rejoined the highway, the chaos ceased, bringing our nightmare to an abrupt end. Within moments the sun reappeared as the menacing clouds departed, leaving as evidence a thin veil of steam rising from the damp tarmac.

Approaching Livingstone, the highway ran along the edge of a plateau before descending to reach the banks of the Zambezi River. For as far as the eye could see we were treated to magnificent views of forest and shrubland. With still some thirty kilometres to go a misty cloud of spray appeared on the horizon, pointing out our desti-nation. For a while it was pandemonium as everyone insisted they had been the first to spot this illustrious signpost. Spurred on, we drove straight through Livingstone, deciding to return and explore the renowned tourist centre another day.

Driving parallel to the river, we passed a warning sign depicting an elephant plodding across the road. As this caused some amusement we stopped to take photographs of the children standing beneath it, as a memento. Shortly afterwards we got our first glimpse of the mighty Zambezi river as it gathered momentum before plunging over a ledge 1700 metres wide into a chasm 100 metres deep. Still in a state of euphoria, we very nearly missed the turning leading to the hotel car park. By the time we were installed in our luxurious, air-conditioned paradise it was twilight. Impetuously, we cut across the hotel gardens, dodging several busy sprinklers along the way, in order to get our first unrestricted view of the Falls before darkness set in.

A narrow roadway separated the hotel from the river and sur-rounding rainforest. Before crossing, we paused to examine a minia-ture museum only to find the doors firmly bolted. A number of craftsmen, however, were still busy plying their wares close by. Several tourists seemed engrossed in the variety of souvenirs on dis-play, eager to find a bargain. Making a mental note to investigate the next day, I hastily caught up with Ian and the children who were already entering the forest.

Guided by the tumultuous rumble of cascading water, we arrived in a well-worn clearing to be confronted by one of the seven wonders of the world. Mesmerised, we witnessed the full might of the Zambezi as it hurtled relentlessly over a platform of solid rock into the spuming jaws of a cauldron fathoms below. Time stood still as we revelled in the magnificence of one of nature's loveliest tapestries, which had inspired local tribesmen to bestow upon it the title Mosi-oa-Tunya – the smoke that thunders.

The next day, armed with macs and umbrellas to prevent being drenched by spray, we set out to discover the delights of the rain-forest. My paperback guide pointed out that in order to view the Falls from a vantage point, one must make for the Knife Edge Bridge. This the author described as an elevated swinging wooden structure. He then went on to mention other intriguing names such as the Boiling Pot and Devil's Cataract.

Meandering along one of the trails in the forest, we were dis-tracted by a series of loud persistent shrieks, made by some exotic creature camouflaged high up in the branches of a tree. By using a pair of binoculars we eventually spotted a large bird of colourful plumage which held our attention for quite a while. The children, having soon lost interest, ran on ahead, impatient to discover something more enticing just round the corner.

As they disappeared from view we hurried after them only to have our path blocked by a group of Chinese tourists. Some balanced on the edge of the ravine were busy with cameras poised; others gesticulated excitedly. Inching our way through the throng, we soon discovered what was attracting so much attention. Half-way across the Knife Edge Bridge, huddled together under Ian's massive umbrella, were Anthony and Fiona. Clinging to one another for support, they were completely unaware that, for a few moments at least, they had stolen all the thunder!

There was so much to see and do during our short holiday. Early one morning we went in search of the gorge where the cataract was supposed to have originated. Referring once more to my handy guide, I learnt that over countless years the pressure of cascading water had eroded the massive wall of rock in a zigzag conformation, resulting in the Fall's present day position.

Later that day we stopped outside a small museum, near the centre of Livingstone, where various exhibits recording the history of Zambia were on display. Inside, we made a beeline for the section dedicated to the explorer, David Livingstone. Here we found an impressive assortment of documents and the actual notebook in which he recorded his thoughts when he first viewed the Falls on 16th November 1855.

One evening we paid a promised visit to the Maramba Cultural Centre and Mukuni Village, both rich in the manifestations of Zambian culture. During the tour we watched several traditional dances being performed by Makishi dancers who wore striking costumes of woven reeds. A member of the troupe informed us that in the past a number of these dances had been performed by the Luvale people of the North Western Province, during female circumcision rites. Although today this barbaric ritual is considered to be a dying practice, the dances live on regardless.

We spent several enjoyable hours lounging around the hotel terrace. On the bottom of the pool was a large, colourful, mosaic outline of a hippopotamus, which constantly tempted swimmers to dive down in order to touch it.

49

Groups of vervet monkeys, perpetually on the scrounge for any odd titbit, were never far away. One afternoon, while enjoying a cup of tea on the terrace, I was entertained by the antics of several of these curious little creatures.

Enthralled, I watched three of them swing down from an overhanging branch onto a table which had just been vacated. Apart from the odd glance they paid me no further attention, so intent were they on examining the dishes and utensils waiting to be cleared away. The boldest of the trio flipped back the lid of a coffee pot, poking his prying little fingers inside in an effort to sample some of the contents. Having little success, the took his frustration out on the cutlery, dropping it piece by piece into the container which he then rattled gleefully. Deciding to join in, his companions proceeded to spill the contents of the milk jug and sugar basin all over the table. I felt quite sorry when an irate waiter, tea towel in hand, chased the culprits back into the trees.

While out walking we often encountered large numbers of baboon. When nursing mothers were present we were particularly careful to keep our distance, having heard several disturbing stories concerning their capricious behaviour.

Much to the children's delight, we managed to fit in a trip to Livingstone Game Park which, at the time, boasted a pet elephant whose name now eludes me. Unfortunately, due to recent inclement weather quite a few of the trails had become impassable. During our excursion the skies became leaden and forecast a heavy downpour. This, however, did not dampen our spirits in the slightest, and we were rewarded by a sighting of the amiable elephant. Years later I read that, unprovoked, the creature had run amok and, later, had been shot by a gamekeeper.

The park was well stocked and we were fortunate to spot a variety of wildlife, including giraffe, elephant, zebra and antelope. At one stage we encountered an enormous monitor lizard taking a nap by the side of the track. He absolutely refused to budge so, eventually, we were forced to manoeuvre the car around him in order to continue on our way.

Returning to the hotel some time later, we stopped to watch a herd of hippo cool off in the river. Through the trees we noticed a cemetery. Filled with curiosity we decided to investigate, only to discover that we had stumbled upon a long-forgotten graveyard. Most of the tombstones bore details of early British pioneers, struck down by the dreaded blackwater fever. I was greatly moved, remembering some of the dreadful conditions endured by these brave young men in the days when Africa was indeed the Dark Continent.

On our last evening we boarded the Booze Cruise for a trip along the Zambezi, in the hope of spotting some game on the opposite bank. This, unhappily, was not to be the case, although an evil-looking crocodile put in a brief appearance before sinking into the murky depths.

For most of the journey we concentrated mainly upon our tour leader, who appeared to be a mine of information when it came to the more gruesome aspects of nature. I shuddered visibly when he revealed how a crocodile would first drag its hapless victim beneath the water to drown before devouring. We were then subjected to a catalogue of gory incidents which had taken place over the past few years. Occasionally our host would pause significantly so that his attentive audience could order a further round of drinks.

Before leaving Livingstone early the following morning we decided to take one more look at the world's most beautiful waterfall. As we approached the edge of the gorge a pastel-tinted rainbow suddenly appeared above the spiralling spray. Spellbound, we beheld the magnificent Mosi-oa-Tunya in all its glory.

10

Our short stay in Livingstone had been most enjoyable and, even though we were sorry to leave, we set out in high spirits the following morning.

Some kilometres short of Kazungula we were waved to a halt by a group of Africans who informed us that they were Tetse Fly Control Officials. In response to their request we all got out of our vehicle which they proceeded to spray with disinfectant. This was done with great gusto and the car was thoroughly drenched. Fortunately we had the foresight to close all the windows beforehand. We were then marched across the road by one of the men and lined up in front of a large metal container. Similar in shape to an old-fashioned bath tub, it contained an unsavoury smelling dip in which we were asked to disinfect our feet.

The workers proved to be a good-natured bunch and we chatted to them before continuing our journey. At their request, we left them enough cigarettes and sweets to tide them over for a while. With any luck another vehicle might stop to be disinfected before too long, enabling the men to supplement their meagre stock.

Going through customs at Kazungula proved to be something of a nightmare. An official on duty told us to park our car close to the landing stage and proceed on foot to the customs building, a prefabricated hut complete with corrugated iron roof. The crude interior consisted of a well-pitted counter behind which stood two young and arrogant officials. A couple of chairs and rickety table, lined up against a wall, had been commandeered by a pair of nursing mothers who were busy attending to their infants' immediate needs. Leaving Ian to join the small queue which had formed inside this heat trap, the children and I preferred to shelter under a tree.

We learned several useful tips that day. One of major importance was that in order to experience as little harassment as possible, it paid dividends to travel with an abundant supply of cigarettes, sweets and newspapers. These commodities really helped to open doors, or in this situation, borders! On the day in question, however, we had a limited reserve of all three.

We soon came to the conclusion that in order to show their displeasure at this oversight, our departure had been delayed for far longer than necessary. Realising that these impoverished officials relied completely on the general public for such commodities, we decided to bear them no ill will. The handouts were never considered to be a bribe, but rather accepted as gifts in appreciation for services rendered.

Any feeling of animosity was soon dispelled as, once more filled with the spirit of adventure, we drove onto the shabby little ferry which was to carry us across the mighty Zambezi River. Some months later we were sorry to learn that the vessel had become a casualty during the bush war. Hit by a shell fired from the Botswana bank, it immediately sank to irretrievable depths.

During the crossing, staring deep into the murky green water, my thoughts travelled back to that period in time when David Livingstone first journeyed down the Zambezi by canoe. Any form of motorised transport would still have been at the drawing board stage. Leaning against the rails I reflected upon the many hazards he must have encountered along the way, having covered thousands of miles on foot before wearily pitching his tent on a small island overlooking the Falls. By comparison, today's pampered tourists could travel by air, sea and land in luxury, with a wide choice of comfortable hotels and chalets in which to rest their travel-weary bones.

Gazing around me, I was enraptured by the lush green banks and riverine forests that had surely inspired Livingstone to write in his journal, 'Scenes so lovely must have been gazed upon by angels in their flight.'

When we reached the Botswana bank, returning the car to terra firma was far more hazardous than previously anticipated. With heart in mouth, I watched Ian drive across a swaying ramp only fractionally wider than the vehicle. The reception we were subjected to at the customs post could only be described as churlish and soon put paid to my earlier mood of exhilaration.

Licking our proverbial wounds, we drove for just over a kilometre along a dirt road before coming to a halt in front of a large notice board, which announced that we were about to leave Botswana and enter Rhodesia. For us this lovely country was to become a haven to which we would escape under the slightest pretext for years to come. As we entered the Rhodesian customs hall a young official wearing an immaculate white uniform welcomed us to his country. Whilst Ian busied himself with the formalities, I surveyed my air-conditioned surroundings.

Through a window, I spotted a group of Africans huddled together in front of a barrier manned by border guards. It transpired that they were hoping to meet relatives returning from Zambia by coach. 'When is it due?' I asked one of the guards. 'Four or five days ago, Madam,' he responded. Seeing the look of disbelief on my face, he grinned, adding that this was by no means an unusual occurrence.

North of the Zambezi, a less than adequate bus service was available to the general public. The one and only bus company's logo, 'Z.B.S.' was splashed boldly in black across each jaundice-coloured vehicle. It was not at all uncommon to drive past several coaches lying stripped where abandoned on the edge of the tarmac, as you drove from one town to another. As we sailed past the children would yell, 'What's black and yellow and lives in a ditch?' 'A Z.B.S. bus,' would be the desired response.

I had recently read how a coachload of students travelling north were left stranded miles from anywhere, for several days, when the transport in which they were travelling broke down. Eventually, a replacement arrived but any feeling of relief was shortlived for shortly after boarding, to the passengers' consternation, this vehicle also came to a complete standstill. The newspaper then went on to describe some of the misery and anguish encountered by these unfortunate travellers before reaching their destination.

Allowing my gaze to return once more to the group of Africans still huddled around the frontier post, it crossed my mind that whosoever it was they were so patiently waiting to meet had in all probability been abandoned somewhere in the wilderness.

Leaving the Rhodesian border behind, we still had a sixty-kilometre drive ahead of us. Along the way we passed several road signs cautioning that this was elephant territory. However, upon taking a sudden bend in the road, we were quite unprepared when confronted by a small herd, plodding along directly in front of us.

Brought to a swift halt we offered a very low profile, well aware that these massive creatures could become aggressive when startled.

To our consternation, one of the bulls suddenly decided to take a nap in the middle of the tarmac, while his companions stopped for a quick snack close by. We moaned inwardly, knowing that until the animals were prepared to move on we had no option but to practise patience or face the consequences. After about twenty anxious minutes, with a great sigh of relief, we watched a refreshed and reunited herd disappear into the forest.

Delaying not a moment longer, we headed for Victoria Falls tourist centre, arriving as planned around noon. Thankfully, by comparison, the remainder of the journey had proved to be uneventful.

We had not booked our accommodation in advance even though several hotels had been highly recommended. At the border a custom's officer had been most obliging, suggesting we try the Rainbow which he volunteered to contact on our behalf. We politely declined his offer, preferring to look around first before making up our minds. As no one would accept Zambian currency, we were obliged to exchange precious sterling for Rhodesian dollars, which left us with a limited budget.

We might just as well have taken the officer's advice for, ultimately, the Rainbow won a unanimous vote. Having opened earlier that year, it was in pristine condition, combining luxury with comfort. Set in a lush backdrop about a kilometre from the Falls, it featured distinctive Moorish architecture, and all its air-conditioned rooms had balconies overlooking restful well-tended gardens.

The focal point appeared to be a circular swimming pool with a built-in bar. Earlier on I was somewhat sceptical about this particular facility, but before long realised that my doubts were groundless. On the whole the patrons ordered cool drinks and the bar was closed each day at dusk, when the pool was chlorinated.

We spent four wonderful days in and around this inviting little resort. Although much of this time was spent exploring the area around the falls and rainforest, we managed to fit in a trip to a crocodile ranch and one or two other tourist attractions. For me the highlight of the holiday was, without doubt, the Flight of Angels.

A few dollars bought us the trip of a lifetime. In anticipation, we boarded a tiny craft which took off from Victoria Falls airport and headed east, following the course of the Zambezi for some miles. For a brief spell we focused all our attention on a railway bridge, spanning the Zambezi. Abandoned to the ravages of time since trading sanctions had been imposed, it was responsible for rumours spread by late night revellers who insisted the bridge was haunted by a phantom train, due to eerie sounds which periodically penetrated the silence of the night. Most of these claims were dismissed by the more cynical minded who maintained that sanction busting was fairly prevalent at the time.

Amidst a panorama of indescribable beauty, our pilot guided the tiny aircraft with dexterity, so that we could get a close view of the river as it disintegrated, crashing down into the turbulent swirling torrent far below. When all too soon it was time to set a homeward course, for as long as possible I craned my neck, loath to miss the very last glimpse of such wondrous loveliness.

During the return journey we flew over dense scrubland, eyes riveted on the familiar terrain below, as we searched out any form of wildlife. Occasionally we were rewarded with a glimpse of small herds of elephant, antelope and zebra, sampling the foliage whilst sheltering under clumps of trees.

When the plane taxied to a standstill, we disembarked reluctantly, aware that, all too soon, our Flight of Angels had already become one more cherished memory.

Later the same day, returning to the rainforest, we stopped to admire a gigantic baobab tree growing a short distance from the main entrance. We were soon joined by a small group of tourists who were eager to capture this phenomenal giant on film. On closer inspection, what had at first appeared to be one massive tree could well have been several growing closely entwined. I still have a delightful photograph taken on that occasion of Anthony and Fiona dwarfed by this colossus.

Whilst wandering along inviting little trails we came upon an impressive stone monument, erected to the memory of David Livingstone. Scrambling down an incline a few yards in front of this commanding effigy, we were confronted by another magnificent vision of Africa's greatest landmark. With bated breath, we watched a finger of the river attempt to break loose and escape behind a rocky outcrop, only to be plucked back relentlessly and hurtled headlong into that part of the gorge, so aptly named the Devil's Cataract.

One afternoon whilst out for a drive, we arrived by chance at the entrance to a small obscure game park. The ranger on duty handed each of us a form, containing an index of wildlife known to roam the area. We were asked to tick the box next to any animal mentioned on the list; also to make a note of any interesting or unusual species not already mentioned, which we might encounter during our visit.

The children made wonderful spotters; their sharp young eyes missed little, picking out wild dog, jackal and hyena with ease. We gathered that lion, cheetah and leopard had all been seen on the odd occasion by a fortunate few, but sadly we were not to become one of them that day. When passing a vehicle approaching from the opposite direction, we would stop briefly to exchange information about various sightings, eager to brag a little; all adding to the overall excitement.

On one occasion we stopped to watch a solitary black rhino sunning himself on the side of an almost dried-out waterhole. Sensing an audience, the ungainly beast rolled over onto his back, with legs sticking up in the air. He continued to hold this ridiculous pose until I had him ideally lined up in my sight, when he proceeded to flop into the slimy water before I could take a shot of him. After several repeat performances I gave up completely, frustrated by his irritating antics.

From that day onwards, when touring the park, we made a beeline for the rhino's waterhole and, more often than not, were rewarded by his presence. Although he declined to perform for us again, he willingly posed for a number of still shots.

As the bush war intensified, our visits to the reserve finally ceased when the park became a refuge for terrorists, reputed to have massacred large numbers of wildlife throughout the duration. After the war we made repeated visits to what we by then considered to be our rhino but, much to our dismay, we never caught sight of him again.

On our last afternoon before returning home we took a short boat ride to Monkey Island, situated in the middle of the Zambezi river. This stretch of land, uninhabited by humans, proved a safe refuge for a variety of primates. Having disembarked, we were soon surrounded by a group of curious yet friendly monkeys who were often far from timid and persisted in examining us from fairly close quarters. Eventually, throwing all caution to the wind, we offered them various titbits, which they seized with relish. At first we were greatly entertained by their charming antics, but laughter soon turned to alarm when one perverse female decided to put an end to such hilarity. Unannounced, swinging down through the trees, she reached out without warning and scratched Fiona's arm. This action had an immediately sobering effect upon the rest of us and we decided it was time to keep our hosts safely at bay. Although the rest of the afternoon passed uneventfully we decided to picnic aboard the boat where we could enjoy our tea and surrounding scenery without further interruption.

Out hotel was only a stone's throw away from the local shopping arcade. Although still under construction, several shops were already open to the general public. The children usually focused their attention on the toy department and when their interest waned, made a beeline for the Wimpy Bar on the corner of Wanky and Elephant Hills Road. Once inside they were tempted by a mouth-watering variety of hot and cold snacks, so tempting yet incapable of satisfying their insatiable appetites.

On our return journey, lost in our own thoughts, we travelled along the red dirt road in silence. Convinced that before long we would return, it was, nevertheless, with a heavy heart that I bade a fond farewell to a country which would some day become a second home for us.

11

Shortly after returning from our trip to the Victoria Falls, the company's Works Committee decided to hold a sponsored walk for charity. It materialised that Ian was the first and only European to volunteer his services. When my husband mentioned the forthcoming event to me I could not help but admire his altruism, and tried to share his enthusiasm.

Over the next few weeks he spent not only much time and energy but also a fair amount of his own money in organizing the marathon. To show support, I volunteered to design a company logo, which I sewed onto the back of the tee shirt he would be wearing for the occasion. At Ian's suggestion I even managed to conjure up a black bowler hat and umbrella to typify a 'city gent', well aware that these items were somewhat incongruous with the rest of his outfit, comprising shorts and takkies.

As the chosen date approached, I became less jubilant and experienced a certain feeling of uneasiness, followed closely by alarm. This was mainly due to comments made by well-wishers, pointing out that there were more enjoyable ways of bringing on a heart attack. The fact no other European had offered to take part should have been sufficient warning, was the general consensus.

Upon being confronted, Ian insisted that his critics were a bunch of self-centred alarmists, reluctant to help those less fortunate than themselves. Although, indeed, nothing seemed to dampen Ian's ardour, I regrettably failed to remain steadfast and repeatedly prayed that it would pour with rain on the day in question.

The appointed Saturday morning arrived with not a hint of a rain cloud, as a mammoth sun took command of the skies. I tried to convince myself that I was being neurotic and must think positively for Ian's sake. As I stood in Kaunda Square where those taking part in the sponsored walk had arranged to assemble, I endeavoured to appear every bit as cheerful as the sea of smiling, African faces surrounding me.

The waiting crowd roared their appreciation as the starting pistol, taking everyone by surprise, launched the contest. Ian, surrounded by his colourful troupe, disappeared in the direction of Independence Avenue, leaving me behind, full of foreboding.

Not wishing to spend the rest of the morning on my own, I drove across town to visit Sonia, a close friend with an easy-going nature. As far as I could gather, she conducted most of her domestic affairs from a large sofa on the stoep. Upon my arrival I was not surprised to discover that she was already entertaining several mutual friends. I hoped they would help to take my mind off my troubles but although I was given a sympathetic ear, I was unable to join in the general banter. Declining an invitation to stay for lunch, I excused myself by explaining that I wanted to be on hand to congratulate the triumphant hero upon his return.

As the day wore on and the length of the shadows cast by the relentless sun decreased, so did all fortitude. In desperation, I studied a small map of the district, running my finger along the route chosen for the walk. Convinced that the participants must be nearing the finishing line, I decided to make my way there.

Once under way I relaxed a little and even started to question my misgivings. It wasn't until I was turning into Jambo Drive that my heart skipped a beat and I felt the blood start pounding in my veins. Giving way to an oncoming ambulance with its alarm wailing and lights flashing, I jammed on the brakes and came to an immediate halt. Flinging the gears into reverse I hurtled down the track after the fleeing vehicle, as if there were no tomorrow. About half-way along Kantanta Street peace suddenly reigned as the ambulance's lights and siren were extinguished.

With bated breath I witnessed the now silent vehicle come to a swift halt in front of a bungalow. Throwing caution to the wind, I leapt out of my car and ran towards it. A uniformed nurse alighted from the passenger seat, closely followed by the driver who was carrying a large bundle. They both stared at me in surprise when I inquired if there were any patients inside the ambulance. To prevent myself from appearing to be a complete idiot, I immediately explained my predicament, which they permitted me to do without interruption.

When I had finished, the nurse replied sympathetically, 'Sorry, dear, we're empty,' while the driver, grinning from ear to ear, shook his head in agreement. In response to my query regarding their use of the siren and flashing lights, they both burst into laughter. It transpired that the nurse had asked the driver to make a detour in order that she could drop off her laundry. Fearing they might be late returning to base, the driver turned on the alarm system to ensure that other traffic would not slow them down en route.

Upon my return, I discovered that Ian had arrived home ahead of me, and wanted to know where I had been. He then announced cheerfully that the victors had covered the course in record time. Disappointed with my response, he retorted, 'I would have thought congratulations were in order. Instead you look as if you've just witnessed a disaster.' Tears of self-pity welled into my eyes, as with trembling lips I explained the hours of anguish I had endured on his account. Any hope of consolation was soon dashed as Ian's immediate reaction was, 'Oh ye of little faith!' – leaving me in no doubt that I had underrated his capabilities.

From the outset, Joseph, a Work's Committee member, had been appointed chief coordinator for the sponsored walk. Without doubt the choice appeared to have been a wise one. He threw himself into the project with enthusiasm, going well beyond the call of duty; persuading several prestigious companies to donate generously towards the cause. I was deeply touched when Ian related how elated Joseph had been when the general manager thanked him personally for all the effort he had put into the venture.

It took several weeks for the various sums promised to be collected. Everyone was delighted when the total figure proved to be well in excess of everyone's expectations. On the morning of the final meeting Ian left the house in high spirits, giving me fair warning that he would be home a little later than usual. Around midnight, upon hearing his car tyres crunching on the gravel, I hurried out to greet him, anxious to know what had delayed him. The aura of success which had surrounded him earlier had, unequivocally, deserted him. It wasn't until he emerged from the shower and joined me on the stoep for a well-earned nightcap, that all was revealed.

As arranged, the meeting had taken place in the boardroom, after work. Top of the agenda was the matter of how the collection from the sponsored walk would be distributed. Several excellent ideas were put forward but it was decided that the final decision could not be made until Joseph arrived. He had left a message to say he would be a little late but would join his comrades as soon as possible.

As the hours ticked away and there was still no sign of Joseph, one by one the other members made their excuses and departed. It transpired later that not only was the missing coordinator a cause for speculation, but the whereabouts of the bag containing the funds was a complete mystery!

12

Anthony started school at St John's Convent around the time Fiona was offered a place at Parklands Nursery. Judging by various friends' reactions, I was well aware that a child's first step towards independence could prove to be a traumatic ordeal for some mothers. Happily I survived the experience with no unpleasant side effects, and rather enjoyed my new-found freedom.

Returning from nursery, Fiona described her first morning with great gusto, having enjoyed every moment. Anthony, though equally enthusiastic, had experienced some difficulty in coming to terms with the discipline meted out. His new teacher, Sister Cecilia, was rumoured to be a strict disciplinarian. She took great pride in proclaiming that she had been in charge of the Infant Department since the end of World War Two and still expected the same high standards practised in those far off days.

In due course Fiona was admitted to the reception class at St John's, under the auspices of this good nun. After Anthony's boisterous ways, Sister Cecilia accepted Fiona's gentle nature and attentive attitude with approval.

School started at 7.45 a.m. promptly and finished at 1.00 p.m. Parents were expected to congregate in an orderly fashion outside the infants' entrance before collecting their children, who were lined up in front of a low Dutch wall.

Whilst waiting for Fiona's class to be dismissed one morning, I cast my eye along the row of assembled pupils. Apart from a handful of European and Asian children, the majority were of African decent.

Fully aware that Fiona was inclined to be shy, preferring to let others approach her first, as we drove home, I enquired if she had made a special friend yet. She answered tentatively, 'Not really. Sometimes Jolita or Nina let me play with them, during break.' As an afterthought she added with some animation, 'Jenny joined us today and she was ever such fun, I really would like to be her friend.'

63

'That's Mark Lombard's sister. He's in my class but is going to boarding school in England next year,' Anthony informed us imperiously.

When I met Fiona after school the following day I asked her to point Jenny out to me. 'She's over there,' announced Fiona waving vaguely in the direction of the Dutch wall. Teasingly, I singled out a cheerful-looking African girl, holding a colourful school bag not at all in keeping with school regulations. In fact, it was surprising that Sister Cecilia had not already confiscated it. When I enquired if this could be Jenny, Fiona replied deridingly, 'Of course not, Mummy, Jenny would never have such a stupid red bag. She then pointed to the only white girl in the line, stating, 'That's Jenny. Her case is brown, and the same style as mine.' Even in those tender years, my daughter appeared to be a slave to the fashion industry yet completely oblivious to other children's colour or creed.

Jenny and Fiona soon became firm friends, spending many happy hours in each other's company. One afternoon, while teaching a group of children how to keep themselves afloat by inflating a pair of pyjama trousers, I was disturbed by the houseboy shouting angrily. When the lesson was over, I went to investigate the cause of John's outburst.

It appeared that Jenny and Fiona had been discovered drinking water from the garden hose. 'What is the point of John going to the trouble of boiling the water indoors if you are going to use the hose pipe? Don't ever do that again, that filthy water is full of germs which could kill you,' I threatened crossly.

'Well, if it was going to kill us we would have been dead by now,' Anthony intervened.

He then pointed out with aplomb that we all rinsed our mouths with dirty old tap water, after cleaning our teeth. Refusing to discuss the matter further, I told him that if I had any more of his cheek I would wash out his mouth with something far stronger than water!

'You must admit he's got a point there,' remarked Ian when I related the incident to him later. From then onwards I had a sneaking feeling that the children, who continued to enjoy perfect health, still resorted to using the garden hose when so inclined. Nevertheless, I continued to have all the drinking water boiled and placed a bottle in the bathroom, next to the toothpaste! Having taken this precaution, however, I managed to contract dysentery shortly afterwards, which only goes to show that man's fate is after all, determined from the cradle.

My affliction coincided with the arrival of Eartha Kitt who was on tour, and willing to entertain those who could afford the price of a ticket. While we were still contemplating whether or not to part with so much money, Charles Lang invited us to be his guests for the evening of the 25th November, when the star was to appear in cabaret at the Hotel Edinburgh.

Everyone dressed splendidly for the occasion, ladies wearing full-length dresses, escorted by gentlemen in formal attire. No effort was spared on my part, such was my desire to create the right impression. Lamentably, this was not to be.

Although the staff did their level best to oblige, service was extremely slow as the dining room was packed well beyond its intended capacity. Nobody seemed very concerned by this eventuality, as an air of expectancy reverberated across the room.

When a gin and tonic was eventually handed to me my throat felt parched and my cheeks were burning. I would have exchanged it gladly for a long cool drink of water. Having given up all effort of trying to be sociable I could only pick at the entrée, which everyone around me described as being absolutely delicious. As waves of nausea and panic engulfed me, a matter of moments after the star made her entrance, I made a swift exit through the nearest door.

I found I had entered the hotel kitchen which, as only to be expected, was a hive of activity. Although I received several astonished glances from the chef and his assistants, no one challenged me as I rushed past them. Trying to fathom the layout of the building, I decided to take a right-hand corridor, which to my utter relief led into the cocktail lounge. Relief turned to consternation when, having almost reached the exit leading to the powder room, I lost control and vomited all over the deep pile beneath my feet. Not waiting to discover the reaction of those present, I pressed on regardless, praying fervently that the powder room would be deserted. Thankfully my prayers were answered.

It wasn't until the star had taken her umpteenth encore that I was eventually rescued from my refuge. The sound of Sofia's voice enquiring as to my whereabouts swiftly brought me back to reality.

Mustering up every ounce of strength in my body, I managed to unlock the toilet door to find her waiting anxiously along with a throng of impatient females.

When we joined Ian and Charles on the landing, I expected to be shepherded down the back stairs and out through the tradesmen's entrance. However, this was not to be. Charles, never backwards in coming forward, without further ado, swept me up in his arms and carried me effortlessly down the centre staircase. Having deposited me in the passenger seat of his Rover, he drove off, leaving Sofia and Ian to follow on behind.

Our friend Tom, ensconced in front of the television, was acting as baby-sitter for the evening. Although I was well passed caring, I could not help but notice his face register a look of utter bewilderment as Charles and I swept swiftly through the front room and made towards the sleeping quarters. Needless to say, he needed no invitation to join us. Shortly afterwards, Sofia and Ian arrived on the scene. Both greeted Charles with a look of sufferance. It was apparent that neither one entirely approved of Charles' chivalry. Thankfully, they refrained from adding to my discomfort by airing their grievance in public.

While deciding whether or not to send for a doctor, Ian suggested our guests might like a quickie for the road. Charles accepted with enthusiasm while Sofia declined, due to the lateness of the hour. I felt completely demoralised when Tom remarked with acrimony that some of us had possibly had one too many already. This did not prevent him, however, from joining the others for a nightcap as I disappeared in the direction of the bathroom.

When the doctor diagnosed dysentery as the cause of my affliction I felt more relieved than distraught. At least it proved that my hasty exit from the Hotel Edinburgh was not due to any over-indulgence on my part. This was, however, little consolation when taking into account the dismal fact that I had missed being entertained by the enigmatic Eartha.

13

One very hot and humid Saturday in late September I had been on a shopping expedition with Ian and the children to Ndola, a bustling little town close to the border between Zambia and Zaire. Although the journey had not been entirely fruitless, I was feeling somewhat disgruntled. What should have been a simple task was turning into a nightmare. During the last few weeks I had visited every town on the Copperbelt, searching for a pair of matching bedside cabinets. In desperation, that morning I had settled for a pair which, upon close inspection, was far from perfect. Ian's reminder that a blind man would be glad to see the difference proved to be of little comfort.

A tall cool drink was uppermost on our list of priorities when, dying of thirst, we arrived home. While Ian garaged the car, I called for the houseboy to come and give me a hand with the packages. When he failed to materialise, finding the front door locked, I rummaged through my handbag for my keys but could not find them. The children, who were clamouring for a drink, informed me that the kitchen door was locked as well. Sending them in search of John, I piled all the shopping onto the stoep and waited for Ian to join me.

It didn't take long for the children to discover that the houseboy and his bicycle were missing. At the same time Ian realised that he had left his keys in his briefcase which was sitting on the dining room table, just visible through the window. I must admit that at that stage I was sorely tempted to follow the children's example and sample some of the water from the garden hose. Instead, I made for the next door neighbour's house where, fortunately, we found her sitting on the stoep. She immediately offered us both tea and sympathy though, unfortunately, no constructive advice.

We were all feeling a great deal more cheerful when the children informed us, at the top of their voices, that they had spotted John, the houseboy, cycling along the crescent. The warm welcome he

67

received upon his arrival ended abruptly, however, when he explained that he was unable to let us in.

In an attempt to pacify us he explained that a sudden gust of wind had shut the kitchen door behind him when he went outside to empty the rubbish. It transpired he had left his key in the pocket of his jacket, now hanging behind the kitchen door. 'I particularly asked you not to go off duty until we returned home. What were you thinking of disappearing like that?' I demanded irritably.

'I was thinking the Bwana and Madam would never forget their keys,' he mumbled sourly, shrugging his shoulders.

Neither of us had the slightest idea where a locksmith could be found. We were reluctant to attempt a forced entry, not wishing to be faced with the problem of finding someone, over the weekend, to repair any damage. Eventually, Ian decided to pay Karl Theron a visit. Having lived on the Copperbelt for donkey's years, it was more than likely he would have some useful connections.

Before returning next door to await the outcome of Ian's venture, I thought I had better inform John of our movements. I found him looking very dejected as he stood under a mango tree, attacking some exposed roots with his foot.

To show him there was no ill-feeling on my part, I decided to seek his advice in the hope that he might be able to come up with something palpable. From experience, I was aware that John only proffered an opinion when invited to do so. This in many ways proved to be a blessing, but there had been occasions when his reticence could have been construed as plain awkwardness.

Before replying, John proceeded to attack the base of the tree with even greater vigour, using a discarded branch to poke and probe those places his foot failed to reach. Having given the matter much consideration, he pointed vaguely towards the roof stating, 'If Madam wants, I can get in up there.' When I enquired how he could achieve this he replied by shinning up the paw-paw tree that grew beside the house. For good measure he knocked down some of the ripe fruit on the way.

After lowering himself onto the roof, perched precariously, he proceeded to remove several loose tiles before disappearing completely from view. In my mind's eye I followed him across the flimsy floorboards spanning supporting beams, as he gingerly picked his way around packing cases and belongings no longer in current use.

It was with relief that I witnessed John eventually open the back door, an expression of triumph spread across his beaming face. When I enquired how and when he had first discovered this unique form of entry, he informed me smugly that the tiles had always been loose. It appeared he let himself in by this method whenever he found himself to be without a key.

I deliberated in silence for a moment, aware that this practice was a definite security hazard. In fact, I elaborated, it was an open invitation to any intruder who might discover its whereabouts and merits. However, I came to the conclusion that it would be decidedly wiser to deliver a reprimand on a more appropriate occasion.

By the time Ian returned, I was sitting on the stoep with my feet up enjoying what I considered to be a well-earned cup of tea. He was accompanied by Karl and about half a dozen other friends, who climbed out of the pick-up, weighed down by a variety of tortuous looking instruments, ready to do battle.

Feeling slighted when they discovered their assistance was superfluous, my would-be rescuers demanded to know how, exactly, entrance had been gained. 'Actually, John deserves all the credit,' I conceded. Turning to him for support, I was surprised to find that he was nowhere to be seen. 'He managed to find a spare key somewhere,' I then added lamely.

It did not take long to deduce that John must have deemed it appropriate to do a disappearing act, for the second time that day, suspecting some form of admonishment would, most likely, be forthcoming.

14

The members of the rowing team were a breed apart. Their enthusiasm, combined with youth and stamina was to be admired, as they tackled each new challenge. The less sprightly amongst us would gaze enviously upon the fit lithe bodies limbering up before a practice session.

One particular evening Ian and I were sitting by the water's edge, watching the fiery hue of an African sun pale and merge into the more sombre glow of approaching darkness. We could tell from the bantering tones drifting towards us that the rowers were packing up for the night, looking forward to several well-earned pints. Ian's voice suddenly interrupted my musing. 'Care for a noggin? The bar should be open any minute.' Not wishing to miss one moment of the glorious sunset I suggested he brought our drinks outside. We could always move into the clubhouse if it got chilly.

When Ian returned, supporting a tray full of glasses, he was accompanied by a couple of strangers. He introduced them as Nelly Nightingale and her grandson, Jimmy. They turned out to be the mother and nephew of Tim, a member of the rowing team. While waiting to be served my husband had spotted them on their own in the clubhouse. They had willingly accepted Ian's invitation to join us until such time as Tim and his wife Hannah returned from their boating activities.

Nelly started to explain that she and Jimmy had arrived in Zambia three weeks ago and were still suffering from the change of altitude. I was about to say that it normally took at least three months for one to acclimatize but, not knowing the duration of her visit, thought better of it. Instead, I stated, 'Hannah is a close friend of mine, you must be pleased to have such a charming person for a daughter-in-law.'

'I suppose so,' she replied, though the accompanying look that went with it seemed to indicate otherwise.

An explanation was soon forthcoming as Nelly related to us in detail how Tim, her younger son, had achieved a Double First at Cambridge. 'What on earth he saw in Hannah Hinton, a lass without a brain in her head, I'll never know,' she protested vehemently. Taken by surprise, I was at a loss to know just how to respond so said nothing. Ian, however, came to the rescue by calling for another round of drinks. With the aid of a couple more brandies Nelly soon cheered up and proved to be, if somewhat cynical, equally as amiable as her daughter-in-law, whose qualities she failed to acknowledge.

We were to learn that Nelly was a widow and, for most of her life, had lived outside Leeds. Her husband, a coal miner, had been killed during a pit disaster a quarter of a century ago. Since then she had been obliged to make many sacrifices in order to give her two sons a chance in life. Tim had obviously lived up to her every expectation. Her older son, Jimmy's father, we gathered, had nowhere near reached the same giddy heights. If Jimmy felt at all slighted by Nelly's less than flattering reference to his father, he showed no sign.

Although Nelly was delighted that Tim was moving up in the world, she deplored the idea that he might forget his origins and become far too big for his boots. The reason behind her concern became apparent when she demanded, 'What would folks back home think if they knew that old Bert Hinton's girl had become Lady Bountiful and employed a servant to do all her housework?'

I attempted to explain that, due to the climate, expatriates normally found it too exhausting to cope with household chores without some assistance. Ian backed me up by adding, 'Besides, there is no such thing as Social Security to fall back on over here, therefore, many of the locals rely entirely on domestic employment for a livelihood.'

'As a widow, I've done more than my fair share of skivvying, I can tell you,' stated Nelly emphatically, lest we should think otherwise. To this Ian remarked humourously, 'Upon the death of her husband, a Zambian widow automatically becomes the responsibility of her late husband's brother. As custom dictates, she must then surrender herself and any worldly possessions to him entirely.' Seeing the look of absolute incredulity on Nelly's face, I suppose it was just as well he decided not to enlighten her further with details of the purification ceremony that followed.

By the time Tim and Hannah arrived on the scene Nelly had completely regained her composure and was busy airing her views concerning the country and its inhabitants. These were surprisingly numerous for one who had so recently arrived on African soil.

When I next bumped into Hannah she was looking slightly crestfallen. During our brief encounter I got the distinct impression that all was not well. Before parting we agreed to meet at the Melting Pot Restaurant for lunch the following day.

We met in the bar around noon and over a couple of stiff gins Hannah revealed that her mother-in-law was the cause of her anguish. She proceeded to relate the following debacle.

Hannah and Tim usually skipped breakfast, so it seemed a good idea when Nelly volunteered to prepare her own, provided she did not prevent Eli, the housegirl, from getting on with her chores. Everything seemed to be fine for a while until Nelly announced that, in future, she was going to do her fair share around the house. However admirable her intentions might have been, Eli was not at all appreciative. On the contrary, she seemed to be under the impression that their visitor was undermining her ability to perform her duties in a satisfactory manner. From then onwards Eli was inclined to be sullen in the elderly woman's presence, a fact that Nelly either failed to notice or chose to ignore.

Eli lived alone in the servants' quarters, situated behind the house, at the far corner of the kitchen garden. Her husband, Joshua, had run off some years ago taking their only child with him. According to Hannah, judging by the number of male callers she entertained, Eli did not appear to be suffering from any loss of connubial rights.

Eli normally went off duty after lunch each day, returning at 3.45 p.m. to prepare tea. The previous afternoon Nelly had decided it was her turn to do the honours. Without disturbing a soul, she made her way to the kitchen.

'I can just picture her humming in that irritating manner of hers as she ticked off each item in turn,' Hannah remarked balefully. 'Anyhow, she somehow managed to weave her way successfully across the vegetable garden, weighed down with a heavy laden tray. It was when she reached the living quarters that disaster finally struck. She had no option but to tap on Eli's door with her foot, causing the fragile structure to swing open. Apparently, her jubilant mood suddenly changed to one of shocked silence, as she watched her treat turn into a fiasco.'

'Go on,' I urged as Hannah tried to catch the waiter's eye in order to replenish our empty glasses. 'Well, at first mum-in-law refused to discuss the matter further. It wasn't until she had downed half a bottle of brandy the following evening that she revealed all,' Hannah continued, absentmindedly attempting to push back a cuticle with her thumb nail. At this point the waiter came over to inform us our table was ready, so we adjourned to the dining room.

Impatient to hear what happened next, I ordered the same as Hannah when the waiter brought the menu. After paying a quick visit to the powder room Hannah continued the saga. 'It so happened that the housegirl and her latest admirer were indulging in one of life's more affordable pleasures and, as you can imagine, at that precise moment, they had little appetite for anything else but each other. Needless to say, Nelly was outraged at such goings on – as she put it.'

'How did poor Eli react?' I interrupted.

'She was inconsolable, of course,' Hannah replied. 'Pointing to Nelly, she insisted the crazy old woman had ruined her life and put paid to her chances of receiving a proposal of marriage from that particular gentleman friend.'

Threatened by the possibility of losing the services of a reasonably efficient and honest houseservant, in order to pacify her, Hannah had felt obliged to offer Eli a substantial rise in wages.

Hannah and Tim organized a farewell party at the clubhouse the evening before Nelly and her grandson were due to return to England. I had seen very little of Jimmy during the visit as, understandably, he spent most of his holiday enjoying the company of his peers.

Nelly would certainly be missed, for her various escapades had helped to brighten up many a dull moment for those of us who had made her acquaintance. Even Eli seemed less ill disposed towards Nelly as the visit drew to a close. 'Mind you, in the end it was Eli who had the last laugh,' Hannah chuckled, before relating the following episode which had taken place on Nelly's last evening.

Nelly, who considered herself to have, in her own words, 'a trim figure', let Hannah and Eli do the fetching and carrying, while she tried on various outfits, unable to make up her mind what to wear on the return journey. Discovering that nothing seemed to fit comfortably, she wailed, 'Oh dear! I must have gained a little weight during my stay, I only hope it doesn't show too much.'

Before anyone else could even consider the possibility, Eli proclaimed wryly, 'Madam looks just as fat now as when she first arrived!'

15

Poor Fiona seemed to become somewhat accident prone around this period. The first disturbing incident occurred outside the servants' quarters, where someone had placed a ladder against the boundary wall separating the garden backing onto ours.

Piecing together the children's garbled version of what really happened was no simple matter as, at first, they were extremely reluctant to discuss the issue, but after some persuasion related the following episode.

Instinctively, my son had climbed the ladder which was to open up an entirely new world for him. Looking down from such lofty heights, he had a clear view of the neighbouring property. A number of hens strutting around the backyard caught and held his attention. Just as he was about to return to terra firma a man and woman appeared on the scene. Without a word of warning the man caught hold of one of the hens and beheaded it with a sharp knife. Whereupon the headless bird experiencing severe death throes, rushed frantically around the yard.

Scrambling back down the ladder, intending to put as much distance as possible between himself and the horrific scene, Anthony, unaware that his sister had climbed up behind him, knocked her flying. Thankfully no bones were broken, but poor Fiona, covered from head to toe in bumps and bruises for some time to come, was also deeply distressed by the incident.

As the children insisted upon removing their footwear the moment they arrived home from school each day, I was not too surprised when a sharp metal object became embedded in Fiona's foot. She kept the injury to herself and only showed it to me when it had become infected. The doctor at the clinic shook his head after inspecting it, stating, 'She must visit a specialist at Kalalushi hospital.'

During our appointment the surgeon, Mr Berkley-Brown, while

examining an x-ray of Fiona's foot, pointed to a minute white line on the plate, explaining, 'This is the chappie responsible for the infection.' Without further ado, he then declared, 'I will remove it under general anaesthetic, tomorrow, and suggest you bring Fiona in around 10.00 a.m.'

Next morning, arriving at the hospital, we were shown to a small ward where several women were in various stages of undress. The pained expression on my daughter's face drove me to enquire if it would be at all possible for her to be transferred to the children's ward. The nurse in charge was only too willing to oblige and led us into a rectangular room further down the corridor.

As we entered I pointed to a tiny infant fighting for survival inside an incubator. 'Look, Fiona. The baby is no larger than Rosie.' Rosie was her favourite doll. My daughter, however, showed little interest, intent on examining a woman who, if her cries were to be taken into consideration, appeared to be in the final stages of labour. Bagging a bed next to the window at the far end of the room, I helped Fiona to unpack her belongings. Thankfully, as she slipped between the sheets, a porter arrived with a trolley and transferred the mother-to-be to the delivery room next door.

Shortly before noon a nurse came to prepare Fiona for her operation. It was with certain misgivings that I waved goodbye to my daughter who, in a state of oblivion, was wheeled from the room, leaving me behind, surrounded by her various books and toys.

In less than an hour, Fiona was returned to the ward. Not relishing the idea of her spending the night surrounded by women experiencing the pangs of labour, I decided to discharge her once she regained consciousness, much to the disapproval of the nurse on duty. Fortunately, my actions had no adverse effect and, thanks to the first class medical treatment my daughter had received during the operation, her foot healed within a couple of weeks.

On the accident front conditions were to get a lot worse before they improved although, thankfully, my family on one horrific occasion was not directly involved.

I first met Maria Pfeiffer, and her husband, Bob, when they called to see if Maria could join one of my classes. At first she was quite nervous and I had to practise a great deal of patience before she would even consider entering the water. Although it was hard going for a while, eventually she became a proficient swimmer and, as I got to know her better, a really good friend.

Towards the end of September I bumped into Hannah Nightingale, as I entered the clinic where I was taking Fiona for a check-up. Her first words were, 'Have you heard the terrible news?' As I shook my head she blurted out, 'A few minutes ago the nurse on reception told me that Maria and her baby were killed in a road accident over the weekend.'

Hardly able to take in what she was saying, I collapsed into a seat in the waiting room.

Sending Fiona to admire the fish swimming around peacefully in their tank next to the pile of books and magazines, I listened in bewilderment to what had happened. When Fiona was well out of earshot Hannah commenced, 'Last Saturday while Bob was driving Maria and their three young daughters to Ndola, the driver of the car following them decided to overtake. Realising that another vehicle was coming towards him and he was not going to make it, without warning, the idiot pulled back. In the process he clipped the back of Bob's vehicle which span out of control.'

At this point the nurse appeared and told my friend the doctor would see her next. Before returning to reception, however, she finished narrating where my friend had left off, stating that Maria and her youngest daughter of eighteen months were thrown out of the car and killed instantly by oncoming traffic. 'I was at the hospital when they were brought in – believe me, it was an appalling sight.'

The three children, who had inherited their mother's blonde hair and good looks had, in the past, attracted admiring glances as they walked down the aisle, when attending mass each Sunday. The sight of Bob and his two little daughters entering church for the funeral service a fortnight later, however, was enough to bring tears to the eyes of the most hardened character.

During the accident the middle daughter had received head injuries; only the eldest child had been physically unscathed. Although everyone rallied around Bob and his two small daughters after the incident, this did not prevent a further tragedy from taking place several months later.

As the New Year crept in the whole community was devastated to learn that the eldest child, who had complained of a severe stomachache over the Christmas period, had died in her sleep one hour before midnight.

Three years later, with everyone's blessings, Bob married Megan Davies, a nurse at the clinic who had offered him so much support and comfort during what could only be described as a catastrophic period. Naturally Sadie, Maria and Bob's only surviving daughter, was one of the bridesmaids. As I watched the child follow her step-mother down the aisle, she reminded me of Maria, to whom she bore such a striking resemblance with her flowing long blonde hair and graceful figure.

16

As a child I was fascinated by a plaque my Aunt Nellie had displayed on a wall next to the fireplace, which proclaimed, 'All the world's queer 'cept thee and me and even thee's a little queer.' It wasn't until I made my home in Zambia that I realized the full significance of this cliché.

Before Independence, employers generally supplemented their employees' weekly wage packet with a small bonus. This came under the heading of food money. The new powers that be, however, frowned upon this procedure, and, as with tipping, attempted to sweep it away along with imperial traditions. Nevertheless, some of these customs appeared to have slipped between the bristles, for they continued to be practised regardless.

One Christmas, in a generous mood, my husband paid John a handsome bonus, along with his salary, compliments of the season. Later, realising something was slightly amiss, I approached the houseboy. Somewhat peeved he revealed, 'Madam, the Bwana forgot to give me the two kwatcha food money.'

'There's no pleasing some folks,' I reflected as I went to fetch my purse.

Opening the newspaper one lunch time, I was disturbed to read that a particularly nauseating legacy from the past had not been entirely eradicated. The article that caught my attention was headed 'The Cannibal Must Die.' It went on to reveal that a local farmhand, Yudeh Nchepeshi, aged thirty six, was appealing against the death sentence imposed upon him by the High Court a year ago. At that time he had been found guilty of chopping off the limbs of his neighbour and later roasting them. The defendant claimed that the axe handle found at the scene of the crime had not been tested for fingerprints.

Filled with curiosity, I made my way to the laundry, knowing full well that I would find the guard exchanging local information with the houseboy as he tackled the ironing. Catching them off guard, I questioned the two men avidly, convinced that they would be aware of some juicy morsel omitted by the media.

Due to a somewhat complicated extended family infrastructure, most Zambians had no difficulty in producing a relation who, if not directly connected, would be in some way involved in any situation considered to be of significance. It was not uncommon for half of the company's work force to lay down their tools on the pretext that they were obliged to attend the funeral of some relative to whom they all claimed to be related. However, it did not take us long to realise that the term 'brother' or 'uncle', more often than not referred to relations several times removed. Furthermore, on occasions I have heard men a number of years older than my husband, when seeking his advice, refer to him as 'father'.

I was not to be disappointed when I confronted the two men with the article concerning cannibalism, for, true to form, the guard insisted that the victim was a cousin from Ndola. With assistance from the gardener, who joined us during a short downpour, I managed to elicit a more detailed rendering of the atrocity.

Phiri, the guard, announced that it was his cousin, Isaac Katondo, who was murdered by Yudeh Nchepeshi of Mpalamatu Hills Farm, adding, 'The other evening, in the local tavern, I heard Nchepeshi's wife's sister say he fought with my cousin because he swore that Isaac had taken money for work he had not done.' The gardener, nodding in agreement, declared, 'Nchepeshi and Katondo were overheard quarrelling in the bush by Spider Ngungula. He heard Nchepeshi threaten to kill Isaac Katondo if he did not return the money.'

It appeared that the evidence against Nchepeshi was overwhelming. According to the houseboy, two other people who frequented the same tavern had witnessed the accused burying the dismembered torso of Katondo using Spider Ngungula's hoe.

Interrupting the shocked silence, Phiri then revealed, 'When the police arrived they discovered sacks stained with the blood of Isaac Katondo in Nchepeshi's house. Outside, near an organised fire place, pieces of human flesh, salt, nshima and water were found.'

Tackling the ironing with added vigour, while the guard shook his head significantly, the houseboy brought the unsavoury tale to a conclusion by commenting, 'Nchepeshi was seen to smile when the judge said the killer must die since he had eaten a part of his victim.'

The next day, I scanned the newspaper for further details of the case but found none. Instead there was a short report maintaining that the Supreme Court had upheld the death sentence imposed by the High Court on a Nelson Banda for aggravated robbery. Banda had been found guilty of robbing the managing director of a local firm, on 14th June, of a wall safe, a radio and a wrist-watch. A value of 350 kwatcha – approximately £200 sterling, had been placed upon the items stolen.

This article left me feeling slightly disconcerted. I could see some logic in having a man condemned to death for cannibalism, but to impose the same sentence for aggravated robbery seemed rough justice in the extreme.

My attention then focussed on an article further down the page, which described a perfect example of what is termed as instant justice. Although outlawed, this practice was still, apparently, much in evidence.

The incident took place in Yasekwa Village in Luapula Province, when a local man, Remmy Chibiliti, killed a cow belonging to some neighbours. When the owners of the dead cow tried to apprehend him Chibiliti chased after them with an axe and knife. Whilst in pursuit, he passed an elderly woman carrying her grandson on her back. He first hacked the old woman to death before butchering the baby.

Before the police could arrive on the scene, Chibiliti had been seized by a crowd of vigilantes. Following a severe beating, he died on the way to Mansa General Hospital. The commanding officer of the province was quoted as admitting that he was in a quandary as to what to do next. He emphasised, however, that the police would investigate.

While on the subject of instant justice, I recall an incident which took place, so to speak, in my own backyard one afternoon, shortly after we had moved to a house in Kalemba Drive. At the time I was studying the discarded remains of a crop of avocado pears, lying rotting beneath the trees. They were proving to be something of a problem for the dogs could not resist eating them. Consequently, they were becoming grossly overweight.

Addressing the gardener, I suggested, 'In future, why don't you pick them before they fall? In your spare time, you could set up a stall by the gate and sell them. It could be an easy way for you to make some extra money.' Before he had time to express an opinion, however, we were distracted by angry shouts coming from the direction of Parklands Shopping Centre. Filled with curiosity, we went to investigate.

At the back of the house we discovered Phiri restraining an undernourished youth by the scruff of his neck. At the same time, with the aid of his baton, he was attempting to keep a small but angry mob from scaling the garden wall. It appeared that the accused had stolen some groceries from a store and then tried to escape his pursuers by hiding in our garden.

I sent the gardener to find Ian who eventually persuaded the crowd to assemble at the front gate. With no time to delay he and the gardener bundled the unfortunate youth into the back of the car with the intention of delivering him to the nearest police station. The hoi polloi, arriving just in time to see the culprit being spirited away, gave chase, hurling threats of abuse after the moving vehicle. Once the gate was firmly bolted, I returned to the house, leaving the guard and the houseboy with both dogs for support, to disperse any stragglers.

Although horrific acts of murder and intrigue were not reported on a regular basis, judging from the pile of newspaper clippings I collected over the years, human frailties were, decidedly, in plentiful supply.

The Scottish nun in charge of the infants' department at the local convent, noted for being a strict disciplinarian, seemed to fade into insignificance when compared to the harridan described in the following incident which took place in 1980.

Nearly a whole class of Grade Five pupils attending Dzikomo Primary School were nursing cuts and other injuries to their head, sustained from beatings dispensed by their teacher. Out of the entire class only three pupils had, so far, suffered no injuries. Six had been admitted to the Central Hospital with deep cuts while others were receiving outpatient treatment for swellings and bruises. According to the pupils, their teacher, insisting that full school uniform be worn during school hours, would beat them with a hosepipe and spiked cane if they arrived at school barefoot.

Over a hundred outraged mothers had walked from their railway township homes to the Regional Education offices, to demand retribution. Although the women were unable to see the Education Officer in person, an official promised the matter would be taken up administratively. In conclusion, it was recorded in the newspaper some weeks later that the District Education Officer was reported to have confirmed that the accused was, undeniably, responsible for the children's wounds. Under the circumstances, he had decided to transfer the teacher in question to another area as he considered *her* safety was at risk!

I do not wish to give the impression that the press was always full of doom and gloom. The following is an extract from a letter, published around the time of the above incident, which I imagine was responsible for placing a smile on a good many readers' lips.

... Dear Sir,

I am writing on behalf of a number of local businessmen who are expressing grave concern that their efforts to keep death off the road are being exploited by fellow Christians. Deciding to forgo the convenience and comfort of driving home from the local hostelry, recently, a number of law abiding citizens paid several youths to collect them, at closing time, and transport them home in wheelbarrows. Although, in the past, this method has always been regarded as a reliable form of transport, we now have proof that this is no longer the case, for these youths are not sticking to their side of the bargain. Lately, several clients have woken up, to find themselves stranded on a strange doorstep. On one such occasion, I, myself, was greatly put out to discover that I had been abandoned in a puddle, in the middle of the compound, after a heavy rain storm.

I remain,
Respectably yours,
Matthew Kapikila

17

'Never again will I own another animal,' I vowed, after the traumatic incident involving Jojo and Amber. Fate, however, has no respect for oaths and promises as I was soon to discover.

One afternoon, during a swimming lesson, I had the strangest feeling that I was being put under close scrutiny. Glancing towards the stoep, I was surprised to see a bedraggled, dejected looking Alsatian reclining under the bench. As rabies was rampant and a tie-up order in force at the time, I made a mental note to investigate the matter further once the lesson came to an end.

The animal did not stir as I approached, but looked at me quizzically. As I returned its gaze, I felt my decision to phone the police, who were known to shoot all strays on sight, waver. It was blatantly obvious that the dog was undernourished and suffering from mange. Its face and body were covered in scars and more recent wounds, while the tip of its right ear was missing completely. It was indeed a sorry sight. While I stood there wondering what to do, the creature got up and, leaping over the stoep wall, left of its own accord.

The story, of course, did not end there. Much to my annoyance, the wretched animal reappeared on the stoep the next afternoon, leaving only when confronted. Consequently, I approached the garden boy and asked him to keep a close look out for the interloper and forbid it entry. This plan seemed to work for a while but before long, I noticed the dog once more eyeing me from its favourite position on the stoep. The most likely explanation was that it had sneaked in with the children when they arrived for their lessons.

In desperation, I telephoned the local branch of the SPCA, imploring them to collect the creature and put it out of its misery. Their reaction was that they would require concrete evidence that the owner was guilty of ill-treating the animal before they could act. Left without a leg to stand on, before replacing the receiver, I replied somewhat irritably that I should be in touch shortly.

The houseboy, who at the time was doubling up as gardener until a suitable replacement could be found, agreed to also act as sleuth. When the Alsatian departed the next day, John followed, hot on its scent.

A few days later he claimed triumphantly that he had detected where the dog lived and discovered that its owner frequented the local tavern. Following the man home after closing time the previous evening, he was able to ascertain from a woman who lived close by that the man repeatedly abused the animal, compelling it to scavenge for sustenance.

Upon reporting John's findings to the SPCA, after much debate, it was suggested that for a small fee I should register the dog under my name. As the new owner, I would then be in a better position to decide upon the animal's fate. At the same time, I was warned that chances of finding new homes for unwanted pets were few and far between. This was due to the large number of domestic animals being abandoned by expatriates leaving the country. Without wishing to dwell too deeply on the alternative solution of having the dog destroyed, I agreed to fill in an application form.

In the meantime I had no option but to feed and nurse the emaciated animal who thrived on such care and attention. Although, for quite some time, I advertised far and wide I could find no one willing to give the creature a good home. The outcome was, that after much soul searching, I made an appointment to have the dog put down.

The kennels were situated along the Old Mine Road, leading to Rokana Golf Course. Although it was only a short distance from our house, the car ride that day seemed interminable. Unaware of its fate, the dog languished in the back seat, enjoying the fresh warm current of air blowing in through the open window. On our arrival, the receptionist commented woefully, 'I can't bear to see a healthy animal destroyed for no good reason.' Wearing a deadpan expression, she then escorted me, with dog in tow, down a long corridor leading into a dingy yard at the back of the building.

'Mr Badger will be with you in a few minutes,' was her parting shot as she left me to my own devices. Reassuring myself philosophically that the decision I had taken was a wise one, I tried to ignore the dog's imploring gaze as, instinctively, it started to whimper.

85

When I returned to the empty waiting room with dog still in tow, the receptionist enquired imperiously, 'Is there a problem?'

'No, not really,' I replied sheepishly, 'I've just changed my mind that's all.'

'Most people do when it comes to the crunch,' she remarked with a self-satisfied smile, as she handed me the bill.

'They certainly saw you coming,' was Ian's rejoinder when, returning home, he spotted the Alsatian in its usual position under the bench.

'I suppose so,' I muttered, knowing that no explanation I could offer would compensate for what he considered to be lack of moral fibre on my part.

The incident was by no means brought to an end that day either. A few weeks later, however, the following episode occurred, which brought the matter to a satisfactory conclusion. Finally accepted as one of the family, the dog was christened Kim, and from then onwards referred to as *he* instead of it.

Dozing in his favourite spot on the stoep, he sometimes distracted me by emitting excited little woofs and whimpers which caused me to imagine that he was chasing some tantalizing fantasy in his sleep. One Sunday afternoon, during one of these daydreams, his hackles suddenly rose accompanied by a series of low growls.

'Having a nightmare, old boy?' I enquired.

Without shifting his position, Kim suddenly pricked up his ears; alert and ready for action. Shortly afterwards I was startled by several sharp blows being dealt on the front gate with a metallic object.

Moments later, I caught sight of John strolling down the drive, with the dog close on his heels. Filled with curiosity, I jumped up, spilling a vase of roses in the process. Without pausing to inspect the damage, I scrambled onto the stoep wall in order to peep through the spiky bougainvillaea hedge. By then, the Alsatian had taken up his post halfway down the drive. Having carefully summed up the situation, John opened the gates by a fraction only, failing completely to satisfy my curiosity. Without further ado I decided to join him.

John informed me that the original owner had sent two men around to collect his dog. Throwing all discretion to the wind, I flung the gates wide open, and confronted the pair. 'You can tell your bwana that when the dog came to us he was an unwanted stray. From the look of him, he had been neglected for months. The dog belongs to me now, I've registered him with the SPCA.'

'They say you must buy the dog if you will not hand him back,' John then interceded on their behalf. Outraged I shouted angrily, 'That's ridiculous! The money I have spent on vet's fees and medicine would pay for the dog ten times over. They can give their boss a bill from me in fair exchange.'

When John finally finished translating my outburst, as an afterthought I added, 'If they bother me again, I will report their bwana to the SPCA for ill-treating the animal, so he had better watch out as they will be only too pleased to prosecute him.'

As I walked away, one of the men, deciding to use pressure where persuasion had failed, pushed past John, and made towards the animal. The Alsatian, who had severed all connections with his past life, flew at the intruder in fury. With a sudden change of heart, the man and his accomplice deemed it wise to put as much distance between themselves and the enraged animal as was humanly possible. My only regret was that they and not their bwana were subjected to the dog's rough justice.

From that day onwards we received no further challenge regarding the dog's legal ownership. As Kim's confidence returned he became very possessive and followed me everywhere, which at times proved to be extremely frustrating.

One day he escaped just after I left to visit one of my neighbours. It was a bit too chilly to sit on her stoep so instead we moved into the front room. Over tea, we inspected a dress pattern which was spread out on the floor in front of us. Our concentration was shattered, however, by the unexpected arrival of Kim, who had cleared a seven foot boundary wall in an effort to join us. Bounding up to me he showered me with affection, but received none in return.Unfortunately he had trampled over my friend's paper pattern, tearing it in the process. Under the circumstances, Kim and I beat a hasty retreat.

The next time I saw my neighbour I noticed a slight coolness in her attitude towards me. Once again I apologised profusely for my dog's actions. With a noticeable lack of warmth in her voice, she informed me that apart from her pattern being ruined completely, her pet terrier had leapt out of his basket in alarm and disappeared under a bed where he stayed for the rest of the day. 'Furthermore,' she pointed out indignantly, 'he is still suffering from the after effects.'

In desperation I sought the advice of the vet, who assured me that Kim would settle down and become far less aggressive and possessive if he were to be neutered. Hoping that this would alleviate the problem, I immediately made an appointment for the operation to be performed. As the vet had pointed out earlier, from appearance alone, it was highly unlikely that Kim would ever sire a champion of champions.

All my hopes were fulfilled as, shortly after leaving the surgery, there was a noticeable change in Kim's behaviour. However, when observing him, from time to time, I was inclined to experience a pang of guilt for I could not help but feel that such drastic action had robbed him not only of his masculinity but also of a certain amount of exuberance.

18

Not all the disasters we were to encounter on the Copperbelt involved animals alone, as we were soon to discover.

I took my time choosing a houseservant when we first moved to Riverside, as I wanted someone who could help with the cooking when we entertained. Interviewing John, I noticed that his references accentuated his reliable, honest and hardworking disposition. There was, however, no mention of any culinary experience. When I queried this omission, he replied candidly, 'I can cook roasty beefy Madam, but not cake.' This was definitely not what I had in mind so, somewhat taken aback, I returned to his testimonials for enlightenment.

Deciding that all his other excellent qualities could not be dismissed lightly, I offered him employment, stating that first he must serve a probationary period. During this time I would be able to put his catering skills to the test. Provided he proved to be satisfactory, he would then be taken on permanently and could move into the servants' quarters. Although he agreed to these conditions without question, I was left with the distinct impression that they were for his, rather than my benefit.

Although under no delusion that John was fated to become a master chef, I could not, however, fault the way he carried out his other duties. Whenever the gardener failed to put in an appearance John would voluntarily take on the role of rustic, tackling the undergrowth with vigour.

The following Christmas, without warning, his wife, Chrissy, and daughter, Jazzy, appeared on the scene. With our blessings they immediately took up residence in the servants' quarters. In the long run this turned out to be something of a blessing in disguise for it meant we had a ready-made babysitter on hand.

John, Chrissy and Jazzy never missed an opportunity to babysit for us, as apart from supplementing their meagre income, it provided an evening's free entertainment, viewing television in comparative luxury. If we arrived home before their programme ended, wild horses could not dislodge them.

We were elated when we heard that the highly acclaimed film *The Sting* was to be shown at the Rhokana cinema in Mine Town. Fortunately, as a precautionary measure, Ian booked tickets in advance. On the evening in question, once John and his family were settled comfortably in front of the television, wishing to arrive at the cinema in good time, we left without further delay. This was mainly due to the fact that the seating arrangement at the theatre was on a first come first served basis. Ian, who was well over six foot tall, preferred to choose a seat nearest the aisle which enabled him to relax in comfort with his legs outstretched during the performance.

With time on our side, Ian drove to the cinema in a leisurely fashion that evening. On the way he wound down his window, allowing the breeze to play havoc with my hair. I was just about to register a complaint when my attention was diverted by a young woman standing at the side of the road, waving her arms in an agitated manner.

Signalling to the girl, I wound down my window as Ian brought the car to a standstill. It was obvious from her anxious expression that she was in some kind of trouble. In response to my enquiry, she blurted out, 'It's my friend, she's in a pretty bad way and needs help. Can you come and take a look at her?' Following the girl's instructions, we parked outside a bungalow close by. Entering the kitchen, we had to pick our way carefully around splinters of glass which littered the floor. After briefly introducing herself as Amanda, she pointed to a door on our right stating, 'She's in there.'

From force of habit, I knocked several times before entering the room. The curtains were closed so I turned on the light in order to get a clearer view. Lying across a bed, fully clothed, was Amanda's friend Janet. Although Ian recognised her as a member of the Caledonian Club, to me she was a complete stranger.

After shaking the unresponsive woman vigorously I noticed a discarded Codeine bottle lying on top of the bedside cabinet. Next to it stood a half-empty bottle of whisky. Bending over, I placed my cheek against Janet's slightly parted lips but felt nothing. With bated breath I tried again and this time was rewarded when a hint of air caressed my skin. 'Phone for an ambulance!' I shouted as I felt a faint pulse respond to my probing fingers.

Aware of constant changes in the official guidelines set out for the uninitiated I, nevertheless, felt sure I had read recently that an attempt should be made to revive the victim of an overdose. With this in mind, I persuaded Amanda to help me get her friend back onto her feet. We then proceeded to drag the unconscious woman backwards and forwards across the room. Meanwhile, waiting for the ambulance to arrive Amanda, between tearful outbursts, related the following incident.

Leaving home under a cloud that morning, she had decided to spend the night with a friend in order to give her parents time to calm down. Although she had tried to telephone Janet during the day, she was unable to contact her. Undaunted, Amanda had gone around to her friend's home, straight after work. She had rung the front door bell several times without success before making her way to the back of the house. Upon entering the kitchen, she discovered Janet's husband, Jock, sitting with head bowed at the kitchen table.

At first, he seemed completely unaware of Amanda's presence. It was only when she demanded to know where his wife was that he replied brusquely, 'Giving a repeat performance of last Easter; she's been boozing all day, and keeps threatening to kill herself.' He then made a swift exit, slamming the door forcefully behind him. This resulted in the glass panel shattering all over the kitchen floor, causing Amanda to leap back in fright.

Reliving the nightmare, Amanda suddenly let go of Janet's arm, forcing me to support the dead weight all on my own. Almost losing my balance I yelled out in alarm, 'Watch what you're doing.' Lowering her voice as though she were afraid of hurting her friend's feelings she divulged, 'Janet looked terrible. Even though I shook her several times, she did not move a muscle. Thinking she must be dead I rushed out of the house. You have no idea how relieved I was when you offered to help.'

At this point Ian joined us. He had been trying to contact the emergency service to discover why an ambulance had not yet arrived. None the wiser and aware that immediate medical attention was vital, he volunteered to transport Janet to the local hospital without further delay.

As we made our way to the car, Janet's husband, who suddenly put in an appearance, demanded, 'What do you think you're up to?'

'We're doing what you should have done hours ago, taking your wife to hospital,' Amanda replied brusquely.

At this the man shrugged his shoulders and watched dispassionately as Ian bundled Janet into the back seat of the vehicle. Before driving away, Ian offered Jock a lift but he declined stating, 'If she wants to end it all, good luck to her.'

Arriving at the Central Hospital, what had seemed like a bad dream turned into a nightmare. Dashing into the outpatients' department to summon assistance, I found the reception area deserted. After a frantic search, I spotted what I took to be a porter fast asleep on a trolley at the far end of a corridor. Awakening him none too gently, I grabbed the trolley while yelling, 'Follow me.'

'Hold the damn thing still,' Ian ordered as he tackled the unenviable task of transferring the patient on to the trolley. 'For God's sake get out of my way,' he then snapped as Amanda and I hovered close at hand, eager to be of assistance. Unfortunately, the porter, who at the time was supporting the conveyance, as the two of us stepped back, followed suit.

Free from all restraint, the trolley rolled forward, causing Ian to lose his footing and unceremoniously deposit Janet onto it. With gathered momentum the unconscious woman was transported down a slight incline towards the entrance to the building. Moaning in agony, Ian clasped his sprained back while the rest of us stood transfixed.

There was a general sigh of relief when the runaway vehicle, scraping the wall, came safely to a halt with its load still fully intact. As Amanda and I held onto each other for support, a swift reminder from Ian that the film we hoped to see would be starting shortly helped to control our hysterical laughter.

We eventually found a doctor on duty, who immediately took control of the situation and shepherded us towards the theatre. As the trolley was wheeled inside, he told us to wait in the corridor. When he rejoined us shortly afterwards he revealed that Janet was still alive but in a critical condition. Waving aside our show of gratitude, he stated that the police would be informed, and suggested we made our way back to reception where they could interview us.

The last thing we wanted was to be questioned by the local constabulary. Instead we made straight for a side exit, hoping that we would arrive at the cinema in time for the start of the performance. Before depositing Amanda at her parents' house, we promised not to breathe a word to a soul concerning the incident.

We entered the darkened theatre just as the director's name was flashed across the screen. Slipping into the first available seats, we thoroughly enjoyed what we considered to be an outstanding film. Furthermore, not once did I hear Ian complain about lack of leg room during the lengthy programme.

The attempted suicide soon became yesterday's news. It wasn't until several months later, when Ian mentioned he had recently bumped into Amanda, that it all came flooding back to me. Apparently, Janet had remained unconscious for several days after being admitted to hospital. Even though the prognosis was far from optimistic, thanks to the excellent care she received, she had eventually made a full recovery. Although Janet, from then onwards, had nothing further to do with her husband, she and Amanda still remained the closest of friends.

Charles and Sofia normally organized Scottish dancing on Monday evenings, in the clubhouse of the local branch of the Caledonian Society. These evenings turned out to be great fun and were always well patronised. Even those of us without a drop of Scottish blood in our veins applied for membership, such was the convivial atmosphere. While celebrating Hogmanay one year, still reasonably sober, Ian pointed to a couple twirling around to the rhythm of the Gay Gordons. 'Well I never!' he exclaimed, adding 'Do you recognize that girl?'

Before I could so much as shake my head, he continued, 'It's Janet, Amanda's friend, surely you remember the night of *The Sting*?'

I nodded silently and continued to watch discreetly for a while as Janet and her partner cavorted around the hall, radiating happiness, full of *joie de vivre*!

19

To celebrate our first Christmas in Kitwe I decided to bake my own cake, having relied solely on the bought variety in the past. The end result was far from perfect, which I suppose was only to be expected.

Determined not to admit complete defeat, I sought assistance from a well-worn book entitled 'How To Disguise A Disaster'. Turning to the chapter on confectionery, I was given two options. Being loath to convert my efforts into a stodgy pudding, I decided to plump for the alternative. Following the instructions, I smothered my disaster with a generous layer of multicoloured icing which I proceeded to coax into peaks.

Ian treated the whole business with great diplomacy, informing the children that their clever mummy had made a special rainbow cake for Christmas. Enchanted, they demanded to take a peep on numerous occasions. Only too pleased, I willingly obliged. My feeling of euphoria was short-lived, however, when Ivy Theron arrived unexpectedly for a chat.

Anthony and Fiona immediately greeted her with the news that their mummy was the best cake maker in the whole world! Naturally enough, she insisted that she should be permitted to admire it, ignoring my feeble protests. Aware that Ivy took real pride in turning her creations into works of art I, nevertheless, found it difficult to accept that my humble effort alone was responsible for the look of distaste that marred her attractive face.

'At least you will have one this Christmas,' she wailed as she turned her back on the cake, banishing any attempt on my part to explain its bizarre appearance.

'What happened to that magnificent showpiece you were icing a couple of weeks ago?' I queried in disbelief.

'Well you might ask,' she moaned, adding, 'If I tell you, you must promise not to gloat, as I feel foolish enough as it is.'

I nodded impatiently, only too eager to distract her attention from my own inadequacy.

Much to Ivy's delight, she had been approached by a member of the local women's institute to give a talk on the art of cake decoration, to be followed by a demonstration. 'As it materialised, the request couldn't have been made at a more appropriate time,' she explained. 'Having practically finished decorating my Christmas cake, I intended to use it as an example of what could be achieved with a little practice and patience.'

She left me in no doubt whatsoever that her performance had been a great success, adding impressively, 'Afterwards I was invited by a group of prominent members to lunch at the Hotel Edinburgh. The treasurer had a pressing engagement and was unable to join us. Before we left, however, she agreed to lock my cake in her office for safe keeping, on the understanding I would collect it later that day.'

She went on to relate that as the afternoon progressed, she had been in her element, soon losing all track of time. When the gathering dispersed it was well past six o'clock. She rushed back to the treasurer's office, only to be informed by the guard on duty that Madam had left some time ago.

When the lady in question turned up on Ivy's doorstep at some ungodly hour Ivy knew instinctively that something was terribly amiss. Over a stiff brandy the distraught woman explained that when Ivy failed to turn up for her cake, she decided to drop it off at her own house, with the intention of delivering it to Ivy later.

The treasurer then described how that night, when she and her husband returned home from the squash club, neither of them was prepared for the sight that met their eyes when they entered the kitchen. The window above the sink had been smashed and forced open. Particles of glass were strewn all over the draining board. Although they searched the house from top to bottom, nothing appeared to be missing. It wasn't until she went to put the cake into the car that the terrible truth dawned.

Without even trying to disguise the note of admiration which crept into my voice, I interrupted, 'Oh! What a compliment! The burglar must have found your cake absolutely irresistible!'

Ignoring my comment, Ivy continued, 'She then had the effrontery to suggest that they must have disturbed the thief, who grabbed the cake before exiting through the window. After the first bite, finding it unpalatable, he discarded the remainder and the sample, as he fled down the garden path.'

'Oh Ivy,' I gloated, 'what an insult!'

Shortly after Ivy left Ian returned home with an enormous Christmas tree. The children and I were ecstatic until we remembered that we had no decorations. Life became quite hectic as we rushed around buying or borrowing whatever we could get our hands on to adorn the house and tree over the festive season.

We invited Ivy and her family to spend Boxing Day with us. Deciding to make it an informal occasion, we proposed to hold open house, so our various friends could come and go as they pleased, without standing on ceremony. When the day arrived, there was certainly no shortage of visitors more than willing to join in the festivities. Even Ivy, reputed to be teetotal, sampled the cherry brandy on more than one occasion.

Sometime in the early hours of the following morning, whilst waving farewell to the last of the revellers, I overheard Karl, far from sober himself, declare, 'Good God, girl, you're on your ear.' Clinging to him for support, Ivy teetered precariously on a pair of three inch high heels as they attempted to negotiate the stoep steps. In all fairness, this last statement could have applied to almost any one of us.

In return we accepted an invitation to spend New Year's Eve with the Therons, who were holding a formal dinner party for a few chosen friends. Shortly after Ian and I arrived out attention was drawn to an elaborate salmon-shaped cake which, presumably, was intended to compensate for the Christmas debacle. We admired it dutifully, but could not imagine why such skill and dexterity had been lavished on a fish in order to welcome in the New Year.

We looked to the zodiac for inspiration but drew a blank, as Capricorn reigned supreme. Well aware that neither Ivy nor Karl had been born under the influence of Pisces, I agreed to settle for Ian's suggestion that perhaps this was the Year of the Fish!

The whole house, having been decorated to perfection, looked like the centrefold of a glossy magazine. Once the pump was switched on nightlights arranged in the centre of pastel-coloured water lilies could be seen to circle the pool in a most attractive manner. The

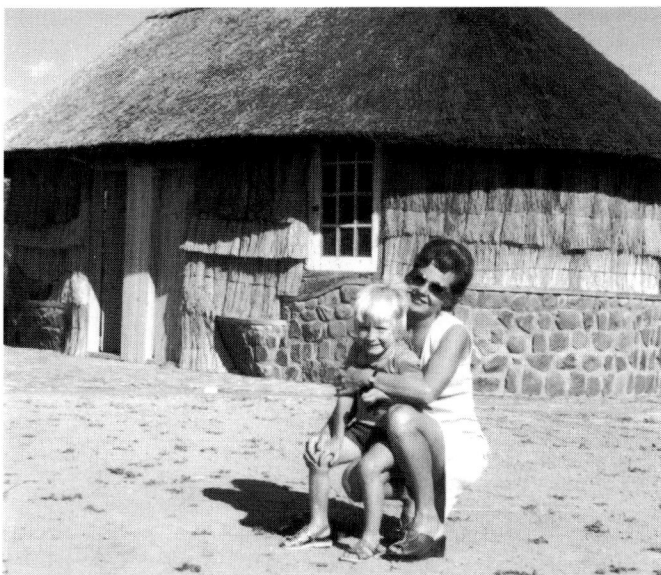

Hazel and Anthony outside hut, Victoria Falls

Our first braai – Orange Crescent, Kitwe

Rodwins – Copperbelt

Anthony and Fiona at Settler's Monument, Grahamstown

13 Chilolla Crescent around the time of the burglary

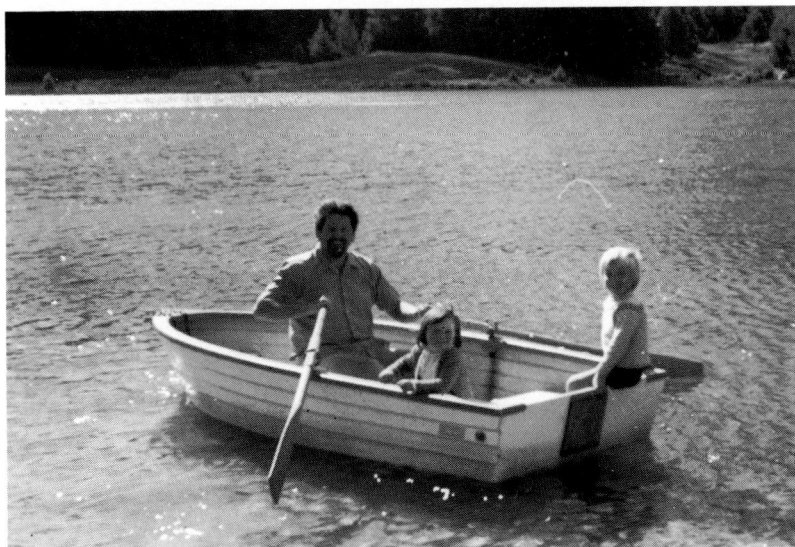

Ian, Anthony and Fiona searching for golf balls – Inyanga, Rhodesia

Above: Hazel, Anthony and Fiona at Wilderness on the Garden Route

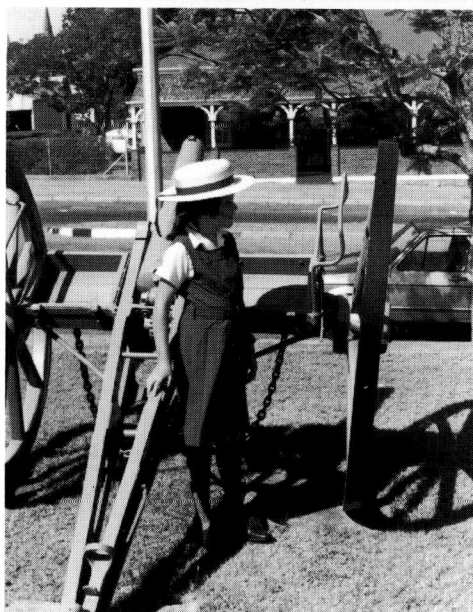

Left: Fiona by canon in Grahamstown

meal, cooked to perfection and served by no other than the lady of the house, could only be described as a gourmet's delight.

Part of the stoep had been cordoned off, providing a small but adequate dancing area. Leaving the floor on one occasion we bumped into Maria Boyle, the lady from whom we had acquired most of our Christmas decorations. She invited us to join her group. Without waiting for a second bidding we accepted, for she was reputed to be the life and soul of any party.

'May the good Lord preserve us,' she suddenly announced, placing yet another cushion behind her already well-padded frame. 'If I hadn't been directly involved I would have thought someone had made the whole thing up.' Once satisfied that she was receiving everyone's attention, she proceeded to relate the following incident.

Lowering her voice, she divulged that she had received a telephone call from one of her neighbours with whom she was on a nodding acquaintance. The woman's babysitter had not turned up and she wondered if Maria would look after her two children for the morning. 'Although I did not relish the prospect, I was obliged to say I would. They are not my favourite children, I must admit. The youngest one seems to have a dummy wedged permanently between his lips, when he's not bawling the place down.'

She paused long enough to take a generous gulp from her glass before continuing, 'I made it a condition, however, that she must be back before noon, as I did not wish to be late collecting my girls from school, at lunch time.'

Expressing her displeasure, Maria went on to reveal that midday had come and gone without sight nor sound of the children's mother. Leaving the house after lunch, her husband, Ken, spotted their father standing outside his house, deep in conversation with another man. Addressing his neighbour, Ken complained bitterly.

The bewildered father apologised profusely, before explaining that he had no idea where his wife had got to. Asking Ken to bear with him for a while longer, the neighbour then disappeared into his house in order to make a telephone call which he hoped would shine some light on the matter. At this point Maria remarked a trifle sourly, 'You can guess who was left holding the baby!'

The second fellow, a close friend of the children's father, explained that his wife had been less devious. Returning home, he had discovered an envelope propped up on the dining room table where his lunch should have been. Inside a note stated briefly that she had left him. 'Thank goodness they had no children,' Maria remarked sardonically, 'or I really would have had my work cut out.'

After pausing to light a cigarette which she had been rolling around in her fingers for some time, she challenged, 'I'll wager not one of you can hazard a guess as to either woman's whereabouts.'

Impatient for all to be revealed, nobody was in the least bit interested in playing guessing games. Instead, everyone insisted that Maria get on with the story, anticipating that the best was yet to come.

'They had taken off with their gardeners,' she proclaimed to her attentive audience who, in return, showered her with a barrage of questions. She waited a while for the uproar to subside before continuing. 'Apparently, the police found them bedded down with their lovers in one of the townships. When confronted by an outraged husband, each lovebird absolutely refused to be parted from her nest. My gardener told me that the police had to drag the women into a waiting vehicle, and that one of the females was restrained in a straitjacket!'

Upon being questioned by one doubting Thomas, she retorted, 'No names, no pack drill, but take it from me, I have it on good authority that both families were declared prohibited immigrants and deported within forty eight hours.'

During the silence that followed Ian proffered, philosophically, 'That certainly puts Lady Chatterley in the shade!'

The three piece band situated on a corner of the stoep, started to play one of our favourite numbers. Catching my eye, Ian asked me for a dance, bringing any further dialogue to an abrupt halt. Shortly afterwards, due to a thick mist suddenly descending, which played havoc with the ladies' elaborate hair-dos, all but the hardiest moved indoors.

Not long after the lingering strains of *Auld Lang Syne* faded, and the last kiss upon cheek or lips bestowed, we bade farewell. Leaving the room, I took one last look at the enigmatic fish which, still in pristine condition, stared back, unscathed by gossip or smoky atmosphere.

20

There were occasions when I found myself envying the affluent lifestyle enjoyed by Ivy. It soon became apparent however, that her life was not always a bed of roses.

On the surface, although her husband appeared to be an affectionate and generous partner, deep down Karl was an unrepentant male chauvinist. The words 'women's lib' did not exist in his vernacular or that of his compatriots. This band of diehards firmly believed a woman's place was in the home, a pigheaded attitude that made their respective wives' lives far from conducive to broadening their horizons.

At most social gatherings, once the cordial atmosphere of the dining room had been dispensed with, the 'fairer sex' were expected to chat amongst themselves, thus enabling the 'intelligentsia' to discuss those matters considered far beyond female comprehension.

This was brought home to me in particular during a holiday Ian and I spent following the Garden Route from Cape Town to Port Elizabeth. One lunch time we came across an enchanting old inn in the heart of the Titsikama Forest. The area was so stunningly beautiful we stopped for a while, spending quite some time capturing scenes of our idyllic surroundings on film.

Leaving the children to play on some swings, with the promise of a Coke, we entered the quaint old tavern. I was instantly jolted back to reality when the landlord stated, unceremoniously, that the bar was reserved for men alone. Ordering a cup of coffee and Cokes, I had little option but to join Anthony and Fiona in the garden. Adding insult to injury, Ian chose to stay behind and chat with mine host, the cause of my grievance.

Eventually, eager to allay any animosity, my husband emerged, menu in hand, stating that as a treat he had ordered lunch. In direct contrast to mine host, the dining room staff treated all of us regally as we feasted on succulent beef with all the trimmings. This was followed by one of those mouthwatering desserts that only a bona fide

Afrikaner is capable of concocting.

Another perfect example of male chauvinism came in the form of a boat trip down the Kafue River. On this occasion, although I unwittingly sacrificed Ivy's friendship, I could not help but feel that I had scored a point for women's lib in Africa. Moreover, it was an unforgettable experience which I would not have missed for the world.

Most Saturdays, around midday, Karl and Charles would pop in for a drink and chat, when my husband would attempt to puff away on a pipe, which generally refused to be motivated. On one such occasion Karl announced that he was organising a trip down the Kafue to take place the following morning. Turning to me he asked, 'Would you fix the tucker if I take care of the booze, Nikki? Just keep it simple, nothing too fancy.'

'Leave it to me. How many shall I cater for?' I replied enthusiastically.

'Let's see, there's Don, Max, myself and you two,' he stated referring to Charles and Ian.

'Sorry, you'll have to count me out, I've already made plans,' Charles retorted.

To this Karl chuckled, 'That's your tough luck, man, you don't know what you'll be missing.'

I could not believe that I was not to be included. With great restraint, I refrained from expressing an opinion, for I knew that losing my temper would get me nowhere. Instead, I smiled beguilingly, as I volunteered to take Charles's place.

Looking askance, Karl explained patiently, 'Sorry, Nikki, navigating along that stretch of water can be pretty nerve-racking at the best of times, especially now that the river is in full flood. We certainly don't want the added hassle of a panicking female on our hands.'

Striking yet another match to add to the growing mountain already in the ashtray, Ian intervened on my behalf. 'You have no worry on that score, she's a qualified life-saver. If it comes to the push she might even come in useful.'

After further debate it was finally agreed that I would be permitted to join the all-male crew after all. When someone suggested inviting Ivy to keep me company Karl just shrugged his shoulders, saying that she was a very poor sailor and would have absolutely nothing to do with boats.

After Charles and Karl had departed, feeling demonstrative, I threw my arms around Ian and thanked him for his support.

'Put me down, woman,' he teased. 'God only knows what I have let myself in for!'

Although the following morning started off bright and sunny, by the time we reached the river the sky was overcast, causing the atmosphere to feel warm and humid. This did not dampen our spirits in the slightest, as we busied ourselves loading the boat and checking that nothing had been forgotten.

Don had been the first to arrive. He owned a farm further down the river where, it had been arranged, Ivy would spend the afternoon awaiting our return. I was filled with curiosity when I spotted Karl wedging a large hamper behind some spare gas cylinders. 'What's that for?' I queried.

'Oh just a few extras Ivy prepared in case we get hungry.'

'Oh!' I replied. Having gone to the trouble of preparing enough provisions to feed a small army I could not help thinking, 'What a damn cheek.'

At last we were ready for off. Impatient to be on my way, I scrambled aboard to the accompaniment of a healthy purr from the engine. As the familiar background receded into the distance we seemed to pass into a completely different world. Max and Don took it in turns to navigate, leaving the rest of us free to take in the sheer wonder of our surroundings.

The river was in full command that morning, displaying all its might. Waterlogged trees, with trunks partially submerged, strained against the murky flow as their tender young shoots were torn asunder. Once home to an abundance of wildlife, uprooted plants and shrubs were swept away by the compelling force of the driving current.

For a while we travelled in complete silence, the river demanding our full attention. The spell was broken only when Karl remarked, for my benefit, that should we collide with the discarded debris the boat could well capsize. Grinning, he then suggested I keep my eyes peeled for crocodile and hippo. In reply I fingered the strap on my camera, hoping to appear nonchalant, though eager to snap something worthwhile. His reminder, nevertheless, made me more than aware that we would provide easy meat for any unseen predators lurking beneath the murky water.

Sadly we saw none of the rapidly dwindling hippo, once free to roam through the forests that bordered the river. As the morning wore on, however, someone insisted that they had seen a massive crocodile sunning himself on a rocky outcrop. I swept the area with a pair of binoculars, but could only spot what I imagined to be a huge tree trunk. On the off chance, I grabbed my camera and took a few shots just in case something showed up on film.

It was well past midday before we found a suitable spot to moor the boat. Exploring the area we came across fresh spoor. We, therefore, kept a watchful eye open whilst picnicking, lest some aggressive creature put in an untimely appearance.

Most of us had skipped breakfast that morning in order to make an early start. Feeling ravenous, we soon made quick work of the chicken salad and farmhouse fruitcake. At one point, when Max returned to the boat to search for some spare cans of beer he shouted, 'Hey there's loads more tucker back here.'

'Just bring the beer,' I yelled, determined that Ivy's hamper would return home intact. Months later, however, Karl confessed that in order to placate his dear wife he had given the contents to some farm workers on his way to work the following morning.

When everyone had had their fill, Karl suddenly proposed we make for Sandpiper Sands, where the tributary we had taken earlier joined the river further downstream. Although we had originally planned to start back home, he assured us that what lay ahead was well worth the extra mileage. Everyone seemed game, so without further delay we cleared away the remains of our meal and were soon on our way.

All cheerful banter was brought to an abrupt halt as the boat rounded a bend in the river. On a small incline, nestling beneath a circle of towering trees, stood the sort of cottage of which dreams are made. Its wooden walls, painted white, were dwarfed by an enormous thatched roof. Little windows blinked out at us from beneath a fringe of straw whenever the sun put in a rare appearance. Unrestrained, clusters of Golden Shower, the most beautiful of creepers, tumbled over a brick wall divided by a flight of steps leading to the water's edge.

An elderly man repairing a wooden jetty which appeared to be as frail as its owner, stopped to stare in our direction. Karl chatted to him for a while, turning down his offer of refreshments, explaining that we still had a long way to go and it was imperative that we returned before darkness set in.

Homeward bound, we questioned Karl, curious to know more about the enchanting cottage and its owner. He told us that he was on a nodding acquaintance only with the elderly gentleman. His father, William Kingsley-Fisher, it seemed was a legend in his own right. Something of a recluse, he had built the house during the days of Federation, naming it Kingfisher Cottage. His son, James, had inherited the place upon his father's death, but unlike his father, welcomed guests with open arms.

Apparently one such visitor was an elderly eccentric known only as Lottie. No one seemed to remember her surname. She lived on a smallholding across the river, not far from the Therons' place. Although they had been near neighbours for donkey's years, they seldom met. Having little time or patience for anyone or anything else, it appeared that Lottie lived for her horses alone.

Rumour had it that she and James had a clandestine affair in their youth. When all passion was spent they had remained close friends and it was Lottie to whom James turned for comfort when his wife returned to South Africa, just after Zambia was granted independence.

Lottie would sometimes turn up like an apparition at the back of the Catholic church, on a Sunday evening. The Africans paid her little attention. Less well behaved, my two were repeatedly reprimanded for climbing onto their seats to get a better view of the extraordinary-looking woman, whom they referred to as The Witch. Dressed in tatters, matted grey shoulder-length hair framed a jaundiced, wizened face. If appearance was anything to go by she could well have been a penniless tramp. Rumour had it, however, that upon the death of her parents she had inherited a small fortune.

Some years later I was greatly saddened to hear that the cottage had been burnt to the ground. It appeared that the owner had been unable to insure the property, due to the roof being thatched. All the poor man's assets literally went up in flames. I could not help but remember its strange appeal and how much I had enjoyed myself that day on the river.

We managed to reach the landing stage just as the final rays of the watery sun faded from sight. In the failing light we transferred the last of the equipment and our belongings to the farmhouse. Once inside, the walls seemed to be bursting at the seams. The front room was crammed full of children chattering at the top of their voices as they dashed around.

The ear-splitting din, coupled with the news that Ivy had cancelled her visit, should have been sufficient incentive for Karl to have departed without further delay. Any hints Ian or I might have dropped in his direction were completely ignored as he cordially accepted one for the road, followed by several refills.

When we finally reached our bungalow that night Karl still seemed to be in no great hurry to return to the bosom of his family. We soon lost all track of time, reliving the many enjoyable moments experienced that day. Our suspicions were not aroused in the slightest when, on two separate occasions, the telephone rang and nobody appeared to be on the other end. It was accepted that there was a fault on the line, a regular occurrence in those days.

When Ian returned from seeing our guest off the premises, he looked puzzled. 'I could have sworn that as Karl drove away, I saw Ivy's car parked at the end of the crescent. I wouldn't like to be in Karl's shoes when he gets home tonight.'

'I dare say we will find out what happened soon enough,' I replied stifling a yawn. Although we still enjoyed Karl's company from time to time, from that day onwards Ivy would have nothing more to do with us.

Some twelve months later I was more than a little surprised when Karl arrived one morning with a bunch of flowers from Ivy, who had heard that we had been burgled recently. Though touched by her generosity, I was hesitant when it came to renewing our friendship. This was due to the fact I had heard through the grapevine that she had broadcast far and wide that all my talk about equality for women was a mere ploy. In her opinion, I was quite obviously nothing more than a pathetic bimbo.

21

One afternoon towards the end of August, I was lazing on the stoep chatting to my sister, Carol. Our sole objective was to spend the afternoon relaxing in a tranquil environment. All of a sudden a large white Alsatian bounded across the polished surface, knocking the cup of tea I was holding out of my hand. Kim did not take kindly to this intrusion and immediately set upon the intruder, causing mayhem.

Moments later a complete stranger, wielding a wooden coat hanger, quite literally burst upon the scene. Transfixed, my sister and I watched as she gave various commands in a refined yet determined tone which both dogs, jaws entwined, chose to ignore. The series of blows she then dealt with the aid of the clothes hanger failed to part the pair still locked in close combat.

Eventually, we succeeded in separating the warring animals by giving them a thorough drenching with the garden hose-pipe. This enabled our unknown visitor to grab her dog as he surfaced for air. Taking Kim in hand I then shut him in the garage while the embarrassed owner dragged her bedraggled canine down the drive.

The terrace had just been restored to normality when she returned. Introducing herself as Mia Van der Merwe, she apologised for the fracas her dog, Skipper, had caused, claiming that it was completely out of keeping with his character.

The name Skipper suddenly rang a warning bell, causing the expression of welcome I was wearing to crumble. This was definitely not the first time her wretched animal had caused consternation. Due to John's resourceful detective work, we had discovered that Skipper was responsible for the paw prints implanted on the bottom of our swimming pool. Having, however, suffered enough conflict for one day, I decided to put the matter out of my mind. Trying to sound amiable I inquired, 'Won't you join us? I was just about to brew another pot of tea.'

Being acquainted with Mia proved to be something of a mixed blessing. Before long I discovered that when relating other people's shortcomings, she succeeded in captivating her spectators completely. I found her performances enthralling, that is, until I became a prime target.

Returning from overseas one summer, I was inundated with telephone calls from mutual acquaintances, only too eager to keep me up to date with various bits of gossip. I was appalled to discover that, although sworn to secrecy, Mia had entertained her audience by revealing a disturbing episode in which a certain Dutchman and myself had recently been involved.

Just after breakfast on the day in question, Karl Theron arrived with some spare parts for the pool pump which had broken down the previous afternoon. He fiddled around with the system for a while before informing us that some part had to be repaired or replaced. Unable to use the pool for the next day or two, I was obliged to ring around and re-schedule several lessons. Before leaving, Karl mentioned that he was on his way to visit a farm on the other side of Nineteen Mile Dam. Describing the famous beauty spot he volunteered, 'Why not come along and see it for yourself?' Having nothing better to do that morning, I was tempted to accept.

Reaching the dam we stopped for a while. It was one of those warm hazy mornings; perfect for exploring the surrounding wilderness. Languishing at the water's edge, I watched hordes of long-legged sandpiper stomping around the muddy bank. They twittered contentedly to the rhythm of the Christmas beetle, forever on the lookout for some juicy morsel. All around various other forms of wildlife contributed to the general cacophony.

After a short interval, eager to be on his way, Karl tempted me back into the pick-up with the promise of a quick visit to a well-known bird sanctuary on our return journey.

Before disappearing into his office the farmer directed me to a small shop next to the dairy. Jovially he commented, 'You'll find my wife, Bebe, working inside. Just introduce yourself. She will be only too pleased to show you around.'

Welcoming me warmly, his wife, as her husband had predicted, immediately offered to take me on a brief tour of the farm and outhouses. We finished up in the kitchen where Karl and her husband were happily working their way through a plate of mouthwatering goodies.

While we chatted the hospitable couple insisted that I return with my children after school one afternoon so they could see the animals. As so often is the case, however, I never did get around to taking up their generous offer.

On the return journey Karl kept his promise and, turning off the main highway, we entered a wooded area. He then drove down a dirt track for several hundred metres before coming to a halt. At the entrance to the bird sanctuary a notice reminded all visitors to register at the lodge.

This we discovered to be deserted. Inside, however, the walls were covered with posters and photographs of various species known to inhabit the area. Before leaving, we wrote our names in the visitors' book provided and dropped a few coins into a slotted box which echoed hollowly in response.

It was just after we climbed back into the pick-up that the nightmare began. I can vaguely remember having seen a group of what I took to be farm labourers walking past the hut when we were inside. At the time, however, I paid little attention.

As Karl lit a cigarette before starting up the engine, the same men appeared out of nowhere and immediately encircled the vehicle. Carrying knives and pick-axes, they were a threatening-looking mob. I automatically made to secure the passenger door but, to my horror, it was wrenched from my grasp.

In a daze, I put up little resistance as they dragged me from the vehicle. Several pairs of coarse hands prodded and poked me in the process. When trying to stem the flow of blood trickling from a gash, received as I knocked my shin against the pick-up, I caught a fleeting glimpse of Karl, who was being savagely restrained. While one man threatened him with a knife, another was yelling at him in a local dialect which he seemed to understand.

Having already confiscated most of my belongings, including my sandals, one of the labourers grasped the crucifix I was wearing around my neck. I shall never forget the look of depravity on his face as I stared silently into his menacing, jaundiced eyes. Quite suddenly he abandoned his mission, possibly due to some inherent religious superstition.

A feeling of complete hopelessness enveloped me as a number of the men dragged me away from the pick-up, towards a thick clump of trees, well out of ear-shot. From that moment, I seemed to observe rather than partake in what happened next.

Any form of protest seemed pointless as I realised that all hope of escape was entirely out of the question. Without warning, one of the men pushed me roughly to the ground. Standing over me, he proceeded to slash the air menacingly with his knife, before pressing the tip of it against my throat.

I dread to think what my fate would have been if my tormentor had not been distracted by shouts coming from the direction of the pick-up. Shortly afterwards, issuing orders, two more men arrived upon the scene. For several minutes all of them became engaged in a heated argument. Needless to say, during the whole process I kept a very low profile.

The next thing I was aware of was being yanked to my feet and unceremoniously shoved towards the vehicle. For the first time in my life I knew the true meaning of terror as I wrestled with the possibility that the rest of the mob might have killed Karl, or wished me to witness some terrifying act of violence.

Reaching the pick-up I noticed a man whom I took to be the ringleader stuffing something into his breast pocket. Karl, no longer restrained by his captors, appeared to be unscathed. I said nothing as I climbed into the passenger seat beside him, this time making sure to secure the door in case they had a sudden change of heart.

For what seemed like eternity Karl and the leader remained deep in discussion but I was unable to make head nor tail of what was being said. Just as I was beginning to think all was lost, Karl turned on the ignition and the engine sprang to life. Banging on the bonnet twice with the flat of his hand, the leader commanded the rest of the gang to stand back. As we drove down the dirt track which led to freedom, one by one the men melted into the surrounding bush.

Neither one of us spoke a word until we had rejoined the main highway. 'How did you manage to persuade them to let us go?' I whispered, half expecting to be pounced upon from the back of the pick-up.

'I can assure you, it took more that a *little* persuasion,' he replied somewhat nonchalantly, before adding grimly, 'Thank God you kept your head and did not panic. Believe me, if you had shown the slightest sign of hysteria they would have butchered both of us.'

'What did they demand in return for our freedom?' I wanted to know.

Hedging the question he replied, 'What does it matter? They won't get away with it, that's for sure. The important thing is we are still alive.'

Believing discretion to be the better part of valour, we decided to mention our ordeal to no one. At the time, however, we had not considered the possibility of finding Mia Van der Merwe sitting on the stoep, waiting to welcome us as we drove up.

When Karl left she demanded to know why I had alighted without footwear from his vehicle. Caught off balance, I replied that I had left my sandals in my car which had broken down along the Chingola Road. 'I normally drive barefoot,' I explained. 'Shoes were the last thing on my mind when Karl, passing by shortly afterwards, stopped to offer me a lift.'

'Now pull the other one,' she retorted sceptically as her eyes concentrated on my injured leg. Unable to sidetrack the issue, I eventually related a watered down version of what really happened. This she promised faithfully to keep to herself.

Discovering that she had betrayed my confidence, when I confronted Mia she excused her disloyalty by saying the episode had slipped out when she had imbibed one too many. Enraged, I left her in no doubt whatsoever that our friendship was now a thing of the past. Although it was quite some time before I could bring myself to forgive her, in all truthfulness I missed her company more than I thought possible. At the time, however, I admitted this to no one.

Several weeks later I read in the local newspaper how a number of mutilated bodies had been discovered in the vicinity of Nineteen Mile Dam. Filled with curiosity, I approached Karl's foreman, Zulu Smith. Normally he was only too eager to discuss any gory incident in detail. On this occasion, however, he refused to be drawn. Instead, ignoring my pleas, he pronounced with a certain finality, 'They were doomed from the moment the local witchdoctor placed a powerful curse on them.'

22

Not much love was lost between Mia's offspring and myself during their formative years. Her son, Giles, was a couple of years older than Anthony, who followed him around like a lost puppy, hanging onto his every word. Whenever I spotted Giles sauntering down the drive, I would be on tenterhooks. From past experience I was aware that, if I did not monitor their every move, the pair could cause mayhem.

When Mia informed me with pride that her son was quite brilliant with his hands, I replied tersely, 'Really.' Not content with my negative response, she proceeded to elaborate, describing how Giles, at a tender age, had taken his father's radio apart. 'In next to no time, he had re-assembled the whole thing,' she declared, eyes shining. Later, to my dismay, I was to witness Giles's dexterity. Given the urge to put his skills into practice, he experimented with several of my son's treasured possessions – all of them rendered completely useless.

Within a few weeks of befriending Giles, my son's two-wheeler bicycle and various branded toys, recommended for their strength and durability, were also written off. Around this time, having left the boys to their own devices for a while, I was appalled to discover the Wendy house completely dismantled. It had been Fiona's pride and joy and until it could be rebuilt she was inconsolable.

On another momentous occasion, having agreed to let Giles and his sister, Naomi, spend a night at our house, Ian and I had awakened to the sound of breaking glass. Leaping out of bed in fright, we immediately went to investigate. Reaching Anthony's bedroom, we had to pick our way gingerly through a shower of splintered glass which moments earlier had been an attractive pink light fitting.

Upon demanding a straightforward explanation, none was forthcoming. The four maintained their innocence, insisting the whole incident was an Act of God. Placing the onus on the children rather than the Almighty, we forfeited some of Anthony and Fiona's pocket money. Unable to mete out a similar punishment to their partners in crime, before sending them home we could only lecture them in the error of their ways.

It still remains something of a mystery why, that same day, I discovered several buttons missing from the three-piece suite in the front room. When attempting to replace them, with bodkin poised, my imagination ran riot. Giving vent to my feelings, I stabbed and jabbed at the unyielding material, appealing to the mystical powers of voodoo for revenge.

I was somewhat mortified when Mia telephoned to protest against the cruel treatment to which, she claimed, Naomi and Giles had been subjected. Needless to say no mention was made concerning the chaos they had helped to create. In all fairness, however, when I met her some time later she immediately volunteered to reimburse me for the broken light fitting. Her unexpected change of attitude led me to believe that, where I had failed, she had succeeded in prising the truth from the lips of her darlings.

Naomi, Mia's first born, was an angelic-looking child. In her mother's eyes she could do no wrong, a fact which proved to be far from accurate. A perfect example of this occurred not long after the Wendy house incident.

Having finished my lessons for the day, I was on the pool side chatting to Nina, my next door neighbour. Relaxing, I dangled my feet in the cool refreshing water, enjoying the warmth of the late afternoon sun gently caressing my back. Catching sight of Naomi and Nina's daughter, Dolly, I beckoned to the girls to come and join us. This they did but refused the offer of a glass of Jolly juice, saying they were busy selling raffle tickets. Naomi explained that the proceeds were to be used to restore the private chapel at her school.

The nuns had been devastated when the large circular building was destroyed by fire on Guy Fawkes day. A rocket had landed on the thatched roof during a fireworks display held at the convent.

Both Nina and I contributed generously. I had nothing but admiration for the staff at St John's, who dedicated their lives to helping others. At the end of school each day several of the nuns would travel into the bush in order to teach children who otherwise would have received no form of education.

Thanking us, Naomi popped our donations into a glass container she was carrying. I could not help noticing that it was crammed full of notes and coins of various denominations. Feeling somewhat shamefaced, I considered the possibility that, after all, I may have misjudged her.

I ran into Naomi again about a week later at Parklands Shopping Centre. She had just come out of a fancy goods store owned by Dolly's uncle.

'Sold all your raffle tickets yet?' I enquired.

'Nearly,' she replied, trying to conceal whatever it was she was carrying.

'Any idea what the prizes are going to be?' I ventured further.

To this she muttered furtively, 'Not sure yet.'

Getting the distinct impression that she was none too pleased to see me at that particular moment, I detained her no longer.

When I next saw Nina I mentioned my brief meeting with Naomi, protesting, 'Don't you think it's odd that she knew nothing about the prizes?'

To this she replied logically, 'You know what children are like. Naomi was probably not paying attention when the information was given to her class. I'll speak to Dolly and see if she knows anything.'

Even though I knew what Nina said made perfect sense, I, nevertheless, failed to be convinced.

At first Ian was highly amused when I related the incident to him. Swiftly realising that I was in no mood for humour, he suggested, 'If you're so concerned, why not put her to the test? Say you had a word with her teacher, who denied any knowledge of a raffle. That should put the cat amongst the pigeons if Naomi is up to her old tricks.'

Considering his suggestion for a while, I had to admit it was worth a try. A golden opportunity arose when Mia sent her daughter around to invite us to join in a family braai, to be held at the Dam, on the following Sunday.

'Oh! By the way Naomi,' I began as she turned to leave. 'When I spoke to Reverend Mother recently she denied all knowledge of a raffle. She thought Father Sylvester over at the Church of St Francis might be organising one shortly, in an effort to raise money towards a new car.'

Watching Naomi squirm gave me a perverse feeling of pleasure

112

until tears of dismay filled her violet-blue eyes, pricking my conscience.

Without giving her a chance to fabricate the story further, I continued, 'Lucky for you, young lady, I agreed that I must indeed have been mistaken.' Then, stating that I considered her conduct to be no better than that of a common cheat, I threatened to expose her unless she returned every ngwee.

'You don't understand, I can't do that,' she protested. 'Giles and I spent all our money on buying a birthday present for Mom.'

'I might have guessed Giles would be implicated,' I grumbled.

'No, I swear he knows nothing. He gave me some of his pocket money, plus ten kwatcha he had left over from his last birthday.' She looked so crestfallen that I felt my resolution for fair play begin to crumble slightly.

Filled with curiosity, I demanded, 'Just how much money did you manage to collect?'

'Ninety-eight kwatcha and five ngwee.'

'As much as that?' I could not prevent a note of admiration creeping into my voice. Naomi must have noticed too. Her earlier outburst appeared to dry up completely. In fact, she looked positively cheerful as she nodded in reply.

Deciding to play it by ear, I retorted, 'I'll let you know what course of action I decide to take later. It will do you good to sweat for a while.' As it happened I took none, nor did I mention the incident to her parents at the Dam on the following Sunday.

When I paid Mia a visit some days later she greeted me with a starry look in her eyes. 'Come and admire the beautiful present Naomi and Giles have given me for my birthday. They are two in a million,' she declared ecstatically, adding, 'always full of little surprises.' Following her into the front room, I mused that one could certainly not argue with her last observation!

On display with the family silver in the background stood an extremely handsome crystal goblet. Attached was a tiny ornamental mouse – not quite in keeping with the rest of the paraphernalia. Peeping over the rim, the beady glass eyes seemed to be defying me to reveal all and ruin the occasion. Instead, keeping my counsel, I managed to smile weakly and apologise for forgetting to send Mia a birthday card. No mention was made, however, as to where the money could have been found to purchase such an extravagant gift.

When Mia described how much she had admired the goblet on display in a shop window in Parklands I was instantly reminded of my encounter with Naomi a couple of weeks before. The parcel she was attempting to conceal at the time could well have contained the much-admired birthday present. Little wonder she had been so reluctant to discuss the bogus raffle in detail.

23

Resolving to put the whole incident concerning the raffle tickets behind me, I accepted Mia's offer of a gin and tonic. Out of habit we moved to the stoep where on numerous occasions I had been subjected to countless exploits, woven around the paintings and memorabilia decorating the walls of the bungalow.

Pointing to some ancient weaponry, Mia reminded me – as if I could forget – that she was a direct descendent of Francis Drake. On a previous occasion I had exclaimed irreverently, 'Not Sir, Admiral Frankie!' To this she had replied contemptuously, 'Who else?'

While contemplating the fading African sun, I listened as Mia switched from one to another of her favourite topics. With a faraway look in her eyes she proceeded to relate how she had first discovered she was to become a mother.

'Marius and I were holidaying on the island of Cyprus, at the time. During those glorious weeks, having an overwhelming desire for fruit, I would visit the local market regularly. In no time at all, I got to know several of the stallholders, who would greet me like a long-lost friend. On our last day an elderly woman, who owned the flower stall, predicted that I had that special glow, only visible in a woman expecting her firstborn.'

Both Mia and her husband were intoxicated with delight when the soothsayer's prediction was finally brought to fruition, with the arrival of Naomi. 'It was the longest nine months I have ever had to endure,' she confided adding, 'admittedly, my figure never quite returned to normal. However, my darling was well worth the sacrifice.' I looked at Mia sardonically, as her hands flew over her perfectly shaped contour while she paused for some form of protest on my part.

'I suppose I could have been described as being over protective, when baby was born,' she then revealed. 'No other person but Marius was permitted to lay so much as a finger on my precious angel. At one stage, I even attached a note to the hood of her pram, which bore the instruction Please Do Not Touch Baby. I was terrified that an outsider might infect her with some contagious disease.' At this we both burst into fits of laughter, feeling relaxed and mellow, having enjoyed at least two rather generous measures of gin.

Once Mia had refilled our empty glasses she threw all caution to the wind, confessing that her obsession to rear her daughter in near sterile surroundings soon turned her into a laughing-stock. 'It wasn't until my best friend Polly took a firm stance that I was shown the error of my ways,' she declared with mirth. She then proceeded to explain that her friend had produced a baby son a couple of weeks before Naomi had decided to put in an appearance.

Mia was delighted when Polly invited her to a coffee morning that was being held for several friends who had recently given birth. This would be a golden opportunity for her to show off her exquisite baby.

On the morning in question both mother and daughter, dressed suitably for the occasion, arrived at Polly's house in high spirits, and before long were circulating happily.

Mia believed baby should be fed on demand from a freshly made bottle of a top proprietary brand of milk powder. From the start she had refused to entertain the idea of breast feeding. 'The very concept is a mere step away from cannibalism,' she reiterated, thus retaining an apple-shaped bosom to the envy of all her peers.

During the get-together, just as she was describing how a close relative of hers had been invited to attend some auspicious occasion at Westminster Abbey, Naomi demanded her mother's immediate attention with lungs fully extended. Without further ado, with baby in tow, Mia made for the kitchen. She was unable to gain entry, however, as her hostess barred the way, at the same time insisting Mia return to her spellbound audience. 'I'll prepare Naomi's bottle while I'm filtering some fresh coffee,' Polly stipulated as she closed the kitchen door firmly. When it became evident that the other guests were taking more than a casual interest in her predicament Mia, reluctantly, returned to the front room.

From that moment the morning suddenly turned sour. No more could she concentrate on being the same charming and entertaining person. How she wished she was in the confines of her own spotless

116

home. When being deprived the pleasure of fixing her baby's feed, she had caught a glimpse of the wall to wall disorder within her friend's kitchen. The vision of all those dirty cups and sticky plates had filled her with disgust.

Wallowing in self-pity, she was about to light a cigarette to calm her nerves when she noticed her friend pushing a hostess trolley towards her. On a spotlessly laundered tea towel stood a bowl containing a pair of ice tongs, a jug, feeding bottle and rubber teat. As she looked up, she was confronted by Polly, wearing a face mask and large white apron. Using the tongs, her friend gingerly picked up the various items before handing them to Mia.

'As you can imagine, everybody howled with laughter,' Mia chuckled good-naturedly.

'It must have been embarrassing for you,' I remarked.

'Not at all. On the contrary, I rather enjoyed all the attention I was receiving. In fact, the rest of the morning went with a bang.' To give Mia her due, she then added, 'Mind you, it was then that I realised what an utter idiot I had been.'

'Do you still keep in touch with Polly' I asked.

'No, she would have nothing more to do with me after Giles was born. The birth had been complicated and I was feeling absolutely wretched. I hated being in the nursing home on that occasion, as the staff seemed to be far less caring than when I gave birth to Naomi.'

Mia paused for a moment with a faraway look in her eyes, before continuing, 'As the bell announced the end of the visiting hour one afternoon, I was in the middle of telling Polly how much I was missing Naomi, when the ward sister appeared with Giles in her arms. Urging me to cheer up and give my son a cuddle, she deposited Giles into my lap. Frustrated by the nurse's patronizing manner, through clenched teeth I demanded she take him away.' She then added philosophically, 'From the look of contempt on Polly's face, I knew instinctively that this time I had burned my boats completely.'

By the time Mia got to the end of her tale, darkness had fallen. The spell was broken by the arrival of hosts of marauding flying ants bent on a ritual of self-destruction, eventually to leave in their wake a carpet of discarded wings. Having lost all track of time, I beat a hasty if somewhat unsteady retreat, knowing that Ian would be wondering where I had got to.

24

May is an idyllic month in Zambia. The temperature hovers at a comfortable setting, producing what could be termed as springlike days in more temperate regions. Occasionally the wind will attempt to command attention but causes little havoc. To those less than hardy an early morning chill in the air signals that the season for certain aquatic pursuits will shortly be coming to a close.

In the late 1970s, when my husband's current contract expired, for a number of reasons he decided to sever all ties with Lechwe Motors. Fortunately, through reliable sources, he soon found a suitable position with a South African rubber company. Although the change brought with it an increase in salary plus perks, I viewed the transfer with mixed feelings.

From the start, it meant having to part with our lovely home in Parklands. Although Ian didn't seem too bothered, for me it proved to be a considerable wrench. Our new bungalow, though not unattractive, left a great deal to be desired. The swimming pool, having been neglected by the previous occupants, needed a complete overhaul. During the sizzling months of October and November the children caught chicken pox and yearned to cool off in the pool, which remained out of action for several months.

One particular aggravation was that nearly every night we were awakened by the nocturnal activities of our Italian neighbour and his Zambian partner. Most nights the man would arrive home considerably worse for wear. Before long battle would commence and continue well into the small hours, culminating in the woman being turned out into the garden.

When all attempts at persuasion failed the distraught woman would hammer hysterically on the kitchen door until she gained entry. As if this were not enough to contend with, their wretched dogs barked continuously, adding to the general bedlam.

Some nights, when sleep eluded me completely, I would climb

onto the tallboy in the spare bedroom. From there I was able to watch the whole procedure.

In despair, on a number of occasions, I begged my husband to report our rowdy neighbours to the local constabulary. Whilst agreeing that something must be done, he failed, however, to take any action. In the long run this turned out to be just as well for, sometime later, we discovered that the inconsiderate pair were close friends of the Chief of Police.

It is not surprising that, during that period, our intake of alcohol increased alarmingly in an endeavour to deaden our senses and snatch a few hours sleep. Fate eventually intervened on our behalf, though not in a manner we would necessarily have chosen.

By the time the pool was back in action, there seemed to be an unending list of other problems waiting to be tackled. Under the circumstances we could have done without the added drama which descended upon us the following May, one gloriously sunny morning.

Although my husband was by no means compelled to show his face at the rubber company on a Saturday morning, he usually put in a brief appearance. Presumably he found company routine preferable to domestic conundrums. Once he discovered the delights of the local golf course, whenever a fixture was impending both his firm and family were obliged to sacrifice his attention and expertise.

From the dining room window, early one Saturday morning, I watched Ian trying to pack his golf bag into an already overcrowded boot. Spotting our neighbour's houseboy scurrying up the drive, I called out to him.

'Where's the bwana? I must talk to him?' he responded breathlessly.

At that moment, hearing the sound of the engine spring to life, the servant sprinted towards the car, waving his arms with alacrity.

I was just out of earshot so could not hear what was being said but, from Petrol's agitated manner, it was obvious that there was some sort of crisis. Eventually, curiosity getting the better of me, I joined the two men.

For my benefit, Ian explained that our next door neighbour had been taken ill and required a doctor. 'Perhaps you would pop over and see what you can do,' he suggested, glancing down at his watch. Feeling less than charitable, I replied sourly, 'Let's hope he's out of action long enough for the rest of us to get some sleep.'

Turning to Petrol I enquired if the Madam had sent him. Shrugging his shoulders, he replied that she had gone to Lusaka, taking the eldest son with her. To my next query, he insisted he had no idea when she would be returning. I absolutely refused to investigate on my own and, conceding defeat, Ian reluctantly climbed out of his vehicle in order to escort me next door.

As we approached the property there was a definite air of overall neglect. The garden, a disorderly mass of weeds, spilt onto the driveway, prevented only from taking complete control by the constant use of a stiff yard broom. On the exterior walls of the house little tufts of vegetation squatted defiantly, roots cemented firmly into the grouting.

Arriving at the front door, Petrol, sensing our reluctance to enter, urged us forward. A narrow entrance hall led into a sparsely furnished sitting room. Although fairly clean and tidy, the shabby carpet and faded curtains added to the overall aura of deprivation. Obediently, we followed the houseboy down a passage which led to the sleeping quarters.

As we came parallel with the kitchen door we stopped abruptly. For the first time in my life the significance of the expression 'I felt my hair stand on end' was, abruptly, brought home to me. Simultaneously, Ian and I stepped back a pace in order to avoid stepping into a pool of congealed blood. Our eyes met for a moment as we stared at each other in disbelief before turning to peer into the interior of the kitchen.

Gingerly, we inched our way around the blood-splattered floor and table. The remnants of a meal had been scraped to one side of a plate which stood on the draining board, attracting hordes of flies, 'The last supper,' I thought morbidly and shuddered.

My immediate reaction was to get away from the place as quickly as possible. Against my better judgement, however, curiosity forced me to follow the two men down the corridor. Entering a bedroom at the far end, I found my greatest fears to be justified.

The room was small and cramped; no pictures adorned the bare whitewashed walls. An alarm clock stood upon the ring-stained surface of a small chest of drawers. Close by, on a single divan, lay the recumbent body of a man.

Touching the cold ashen temple with my fingertips, I probed, in vain, for some sign of life as I gazed into a pair of lustreless grey eyes. From the foot of the bed Ian inquired if he could be of any assistance. Turning towards him I laughed nervously, before stating, 'Unless you're capable of performing miracles, there's little anyone can do.'

Breaking the shocked silence, the alarm clock suddenly began to ring. Taken by surprise, I glanced at the timeworn face, distorted by a large crack. I found myself musing sceptically whether the clock alone had witnessed the approach of death whilst ticking away the final moments of the man's life.

Whilst Ian returned to the front room to telephone for assistance, Petrol showed me to another bedroom where Dino, the younger son, was fast asleep. The toddler awoke as we entered and I helped him to dress while Petrol packed a small bag with a few of the boy's belongings. Although our children had spoken to the two brothers from time to time, I had only waved to them from a distance. Surprisingly, Dino put up no resistance and took my hand when I asked him if he would like to come and stay with us for a while.

As we left the house Ian told Petrol on no account to wander off, in case the police should want to question him. Petrol nodded reluctantly before disappearing around the back of the house. I imagine he did not relish the thought of being interrogated by the local constabulary, who were reputed to use some very persuasive methods in order to unearth the truth.

We had learnt very little concerning our neighbour's last hours from his servant. It appeared that when he arrived early that morning, he had found his master lying on the kitchen floor. When the unfortunate man regained consciousness, he maintained that shortly after finishing supper, he had fallen and hit his head on the corner of the table. He must have lain there all night. 'First I helped Bwana into the bedroom and then came to get you,' Petrol alleged before laying the subject to rest. Although I had seen no sign of a wound and had my doubts, I certainly had no intention of examining the dead man's head to check his story. Any further probing I preferred to leave to the experts.

In our wisdom, we assumed that once we had informed the police and medical authorities of the matter the whole affair would be taken completely out of our hands. The doctor whom the local clinic advised my husband to contact informed Ian that he was not on duty and cut him off abruptly before any form of protest could be registered. Furthermore, he fared little better when he telephoned the local police station, where the officer on duty proved to be aggressive and arrogant. Eventually, he agreed to go in search of a senior official, keeping Ian waiting for what seemed to be an eternity.

When the sergeant in charge eventually responded he was even more belligerent, demanding that my husband transport the corpse to the police station without further delay. Well aware that Ian was not noted for thwarting the voice of authority, I was amazed to hear him bellow down the mouthpiece, 'Like hell I will!'

The officer in question had not mellowed in the slightest when my husband arrived empty-handed some time later. Trying to pacify the enraged man, Ian suggested that he could drive the officer back to the dead man's house, from where the body could then be transported by the police in the pick-up, belonging to the dead man, which was parked in his driveway.

This bit of logic, unfortunately, did not appear to placate the man in the slightest. If anything, it seemed to aggravate the situation. Thankfully, before any real harm was done, two officers from the CID presented themselves, dismissing Ian's interrogators. My husband then spent the best part of two hours relating all the facts for their benefit. The outcome was that they commandeered both Ian's car and the pick-up for an unlimited period.

Ian was definitely not at his best when he returned home later that day, having experienced the harrowing ordeal of assisting the police in transporting the corpse to the local mortuary. From there he had been ordered to collect and deliver Petrol to the police station. The only silver lining to that particular cloud was that Ian's car, somewhat the worse for wear, was restored to its rightful owner during the following week.

25

It came as no great surprise to me that the tragic event of the death of our neighbour did not end there and then. A few days later, peering over the garden wall, I spotted Petrol relaxing on the kitchen steps, teasing the dogs with a chicken bone. By his presence, I gathered the police had been less than successful in extracting any further information and had consequently accepted his interpretation of the incident.

Since that fateful day, the quality of our life had improved immensely. Even the dogs, sensing something was amiss kept their howling to a minimum, enabling us to get a decent night's rest. During the day, however, a group of hired mourners planted themselves outside our neighbour's front door and, true to tradition, set up a dreadful din, weeping and wailing from dawn until dusk.

During this period Dino played contentedly with our children, who took to him immediately. He was an undemanding little fellow, a joy to be with. Our houseboy, John, however, did not share our sentiments and was greatly put out when he discovered we had invited Dino to stay in our home. 'But Madam,' he entreated, with large doleful eyes, 'that child will bring much trouble into this house. Send him home before it is too late.'

When he realised that his pleas were falling on deaf ears John became morose and forbade his wife and son to enter our bungalow. He stuck to his resolution relentlessly and no one could persuade him otherwise, until Dino's mother, Josephine, returning home unexpectedly, sent Petrol to collect her son.

I put it down to grief mixed with a tinge of guilt that the boy's mother failed to claim Dino in person. It was with a sense of loss that I packed the child's few belongings before handing him over to Petrol. Needless to say, none of us suffered any ill effects from his visit, and we were sorry to see him leave.

Life soon returned to normal and though not forgotten, May's tragedy became yesterday's news. Although, from all accounts, our neighbour had been an eminent member of the local Italian community, the media had shown little if any interest in his demise. However, on the day of the funeral, I spotted a single insertion in the bereavement column, which revealed that Frank Zitelli had passed away a few weeks before his forty third birthday.

When Soyashi entered the kitchen one morning, I believed John had eventually forgiven me for risking the welfare of himself and his family. Later that same day he announced that there was a policeman at the front door asking to see me. I detected a look of malice in John's eyes as he added, 'He will not come inside the house,' as if that in itself were a sign of impending doom. Dismissing John with an air of nonchalance, I could have done with Ian's support as I went to confront my visitor. The inspector wore an arrogant expression as he introduced himself and I tried not to feel intimidated. Putting all niceties aside, he declined my invitation to step indoors, saying that he had an appointment with the District Governor shortly, and did not wish to be late.

He then demanded to know if I were the person responsible for removing the small boy from the house next door, on the day of his father's death.

'Surely you are not accusing me of kidnapping Dino?' I gasped in astonishment.

At this a hint of amusement crossed his handsome lean face. 'Please let me explain. I happen to be a close friend of the Zitelli family, and am here to thank you for looking after the child during such a trying period.'

He then mentioned that the pathologist's report had stated that my neighbour had died from a massive heart attack. 'Mr Zitelli was rather inclined to burn the candle at both ends, so I suppose it was inevitable,' he concluded. Saluting smartly, he thanked me once again before departing. It was with mixed feelings that I watched him stride down the drive towards his chauffeur-driven vehicle.

The following Sunday we had been invited to a midday *braai* by the local vicar and his wife. I was looking forward to the occasion on two accounts. Firstly, they were extremely hospitable. Secondly, it meant I did not have to prepare Sunday lunch and could idle the morning away, relaxing by the side of the pool.

Ian was in the process of preventing the children adding frog spawn to the chlorinated water when someone banged on the front gate. Leaving Ian and frogs to their own devices, Anthony and Fiona tore down the drive to investigate with dogs in tow, barking furiously. 'It's Petrol,' they yelled above the din. Normally, we did not appreciate uninvited guests at the weekend, but in this case we were intrigued to learn that Dino's mother intended paying us a visit.

Shortly afterwards, she arrived on the scene, accompanied by an extremely smart, middle-aged gentleman. He introduced himself as Mario Zitelli, the brother of the late Frank. Madam Zitelli, whom the stranger called Josephine, curtseyed politely before taking a seat. As far as I can remember, she uttered not a single word during the whole visit, but smiled amiably from time to time.

Once we had exchanged a few pleasantries Mario proceeded to explain the purpose of his visit. With no holes barred, he related how the discovery of Josephine and her two small sons had come as an added shock. 'It will not be easy breaking the news to the rest of my family. Frank already has a wife in Italy, and although they have lived apart for some time, there has never been any mention of a divorce. We are devout Roman Catholics you understand,' he stipulated in order to clarify the position.

I glanced briefly at Josephine for some response but none was forthcoming. Instead she sipped her coffee unemotionally with eyes downcast. One could have mistaken her for being an impartial bystander, rather than directly involved in the affair. Following my gaze Mario continued, 'I am making arrangements for the children and their mother to accompany me when I return to Italy, with Frank's body, next week.' Somehow, the thought of Josephine fitting into a conservative, middle class Italian background seemed highly improbable.

Waving aside the offer of something a little stronger than the now cold cup of coffee at his elbow Mario expounded, 'The death certificate alleges that my brother died of a heart attack. I find this incredible for he was a relatively young man who, I was led to believe, enjoyed good health. When Josephine told me of your involvement, I was eager to meet you, hoping that you might be able to throw some light on the matter.'

While I racked my brain for the right words, Ian replied sympathetically, 'I'm sorry but I can't add anything to what you already know, but if it is of any help, we are both under the impression that Frank died peacefully in his sleep.'

Both Ian and I, it seemed, were of the opinion that Mario had enough problems as it was, without our adding to them by encouraging him to antagonise the police with unfounded suspicions and doubts. After all, nobody had positive proof that Frank had died from anything else but a heart attack.

After what can only be described as an uncomfortable silence, Mario uttered forlornly, 'Josephine is so young, she and my brother must have been very much in love, wouldn't you say?' I nodded in response while recalling past passionate performances which could hardly have been termed as endearing. Grateful for the distraction, I readily accepted the cigarette he offered me, momentarily forgetting my recent resolution to break the habit.

From that day onwards we never set eyes on the Zitelli family again. There were moments, nevertheless, when I would stop to wonder how Josephine was coping with her new in-laws so far away from home.

The following month a Swedish couple moved into the bungalow next door. Occasionally, our peace would be shattered by their record player working overtime. Our new neighbours appeared to possess a never-ending collection of Abba recordings which, before long, we came to know and enjoy. As a matter of fact, by the time we left Solwezi Avenue, our entire family had become ardent fans.

26

During the period when our nights were being constantly disturbed by the midnight manoeuvres of our next door neighbours, Ian and I discussed the possibility of moving house. At that time, however, property on the Copperbelt was at a premium so the chances of finding suitable, alternative, accommodation were practically impossible.

It was not until several months after Frank's death that I learnt that a bungalow in Jacaranda Crescent, which we had so often admired, was about to be put on the market. Still wishing to escape from our present surroundings, Ian persuaded his company to put in an offer which was eventually accepted.

Rumour had it that, some time ago, the owner had disappeared in mysterious circumstances. Shortly afterwards his wife found consolation with a man nearly half her age who she eventually invited to take up permanent residence. The two made a handsome pair and, if appearance was anything to go by, they were devoted to one another. Although they kept themselves very much to themselves it somehow became common knowledge that the couple were considering severing all ties with the past by taking up residence down south.

Naturally, I was delighted the day Ian arrived home with news that there was every possibility, before long, we would be moving into the spacious bungalow. However, little did I realise at the time, that it could well have been a case of jumping out of the frying pan into the fire.

After a tour of inspection I was convinced that the property, described as highly desirable, would make a perfect home in which we could live and entertain our friends. The back garden, however, was a completely different matter. A circular swimming pool, though in good working order, had been sadly neglected. The vegetable garden and flower beds, overgrown and choked by weeds, were a definite eyesore. 'Don't worry,' the agent assured us as a note of

127

disapproval crept into Ian's voice. 'A couple of strong labourers and a few trips to the garden centre will soon sort that out.'

It was eventually agreed that the agent's firm would meet some of the cost towards restoring the garden to its former glory. For his part, Ian would select a number of trees and shrubs from a specified nursery and also provide and supervise the labour force.

From then onwards, I lived only for the moment when we would move to Jacaranda Crescent. I spent hours planning how I would furnish and arrange each room, chopping and changing from one design and colour scheme to another.

Therefore it came as a shattering blow, one evening, when quite out of the blue Ian mentioned that my plans might have to be shelved indefinitely. Once I had got over the initial shock, he proceeded to relate what he termed as being one of the most traumatic ordeals it had ever been his misfortune to encounter.

He had left the factory early that afternoon in order to supervise the planting of a row of saplings in the garden of what was to be our new home. His friend, Charles Lang, who had moved to Johannesburg and was visiting the Copperbelt for a few days, offered to give him a hand. When my husband arrived Charles was already supervising the digging.

'How are things going?' Ian enquired with enthusiasm.

'Fine – couldn't be better,' Charles emphasised, inevitably tempting fate in the process.

The caretaker on duty introduced himself as Patson. It appeared that he came from the same township as the two labourers, busy hacking away at the weeds and rubble. Without further ado he discarded his jacket, cheerfully lending a hand when the going got tough. Stopping for a break, the man announced proudly, 'Before Madam left, she got me a job down the mine, and a house in the compound to go with it. I finish with Securiguard at the end of the month.'

For a while the men all toiled away amicably to the constant demands of Charles and Ian. It wasn't until they were planting the very last sapling, a flamboyant, that the situation deteriorated. 'The hole needs widening more to the left, or the roots will be damaged,' Charles insisted. 'Bwana must not dig there,' the caretaker suddenly intervened, wearing a look of consternation. When questioned, he examined the hole thoughtfully for a while. 'Water pipes,' he suddenly divulged.

'Rubbish man, they are nowhere near here,' Ian declared, and turning to the labourers, instructed them to continue.

The two men wielded their spades with added vigour as a disgruntled Patson watched from the sideline. 'That will do,' Charles directed, as one of the men threw down his shovel and started scraping away the soil with his bare hands. Assisted by his companion he then carefully eased a roll of sacking to the surface. 'Take it into the shade,' Ian indicated, pointing to a jacaranda close by.

Gingerly picking their way, the two men made for the tree, followed closely by the others, impatient to discover what had been unearthed. 'From the look on their faces you would think they were carrying a dead body,' Ian remarked jokingly. Unable to appreciate such humour, the bearers, immediately dropped the bundle, dispersing the contents at his feet. Several bones, including a skull which stared up through eyeless sockets, caused the onlookers to step back a pace or two.

Following a prolonged silence, pulling himself together, Ian stated, ' I suppose the police should be informed.' This announcement acted as an immediate stimulant. Dropping to his knees the caretaker pleaded, 'Don't bring the police, Bwana, they will beat the soles of our feet and have us thrown into prison.' At the very thought of being subjected to such torment the man began to tremble, and looking heavenwards, called upon the Almighty for protection.

The two other men, having had time to reflect upon the intricacy of their traditional upbringing, pleaded, 'We must put the bones back now now, Bwana. If the spirit is disturbed it will return to haunt us.' Intervening on their behalf the caretaker, still shaken, insisted that this was indeed the case, predicting that all of them would most certainly be doomed.

Taking Ian aside, Charles pointed out that once the police were involved, not only would the caretaker become a victim of instant justice, but there was a strong possibility that all of them would be marched to the station to be interrogated for hours on end.

After further debate, turning to the three Africans, Charles remarked disparagingly, 'Come on, we've wasted enough time

129

already, they are probably the bones of some old animal buried by its owner, in the garden, years ago.'

'The bwana is right,' the caretaker postulated, all signs of remorse evaporating. Staring into the newly dug hole for inspiration he then testified, ' I remember Madam had the gardener bury a dog here, some time ago.'

'Then you'd better hurry, man, and get the lot back before its spirit grabs you,' Charles jested. Without further delay, the three men returned the scattered remains to the makeshift grave.

From then onwards the dream bungalow seemed to lose its appeal for both of us. It was, therefore, with some reluctance that Ian and I decided to stay put and wait for alternative accommodation to come onto the market.

Not long afterwards the firm's spare parts manager moved to the bungalow in Jacaranda Crescent. Once his family had settled in, Ian and I were invited to a housewarming party. Being of a superstitious nature, I decided to give them a small icon which I had been told had been blessed by the Pope. Its presence, I reasoned, might help to ward off any evil spirits should the need arise. Completely unaware of the motive behind my choice of gift, the couple appeared to be delighted with what they claimed to be a novel if somewhat unusual housewarming present.

We soon forgot the incident until a couple of years later, when the whole unfortunate business came flooding back. Opening the local newspaper one morning, an article on the bottom of the front page caught my eye. It described how Patson Mgabwe, a local miner, had been crushed to death by a mechanical digger at the opencast mine along the Chingola Road. A small picture accompanied the insertion. Looking at the ex-caretaker's smiling face, I felt a tinge of sadness, and hoped that he – and those mysterious remains – would be granted eternal rest.

27

In retrospect, I sometimes wondered if I had been a trifle hasty in parting with my precious icon. It appeared that its present owners seemed to be in little need of any protective powers. On the other hand, having escaped from Solwezi Avenue and once installed in our new home, we seemed to experience one catastrophe after another.

Originally, 13 Chilolla Crescent had been acquired to accommodate the managing director and his family. Before moving in, however, they had second thoughts and turned it down, preferring to live in a large bungalow on a couple of acres of land out at Garneton.

My first impression of the rejected dwelling had been one of sheer delight. Through a pair of heavily secured wrought iron gates I had caught a glimpse of the enchanting homestead, which peeped through blue flowering jacarandas straddling the twisting driveway. On either side sprinklers pirouetted across lawns dotted with crimson-leafed poinsettias, flowering harmoniously amidst a variety of rose trees and similar shrubs.

Directly in front of the split-level dwelling, the driveway opened onto a courtyard. A massive carport claimed most of the ground floor area to the right. On closer inspection, through a small porthole next to the front door, one could make out a mahogany bar tucked neatly under a flight of stairs which spiralled upwards.

At one end of the courtyard handhewn steps disappeared behind a wall screened with bougainvillaea. Behind this colourful tapestry lay a small orchard where lychee and various citrus trees grew in profusion, eager to encroach upon the kitchen garden beyond.

To the rear of the carport a solid wall of rock was punctuated by a stout wooden door. Within its confines lay a labyrinth of passages. These, we learned later, led to several musky, dank cellars which discouraged all who dared to trespass. Further along the wall a huge pair of 'elephant ears' stood guard before a steep flight of steps which led to the pool area, at the back of the house.

When we first toured the property two turtledoves had flown over-head before settling upon the chimney stack. From this vantage point they were partially hidden by a flowery mass of golden shower which, in a blaze of glory, cascaded recklessly onto fiery granite walls. Overcome by emotion, I convinced myself that this was a symbol that we were, at last, to enjoy both peace and contentment.

28

Life appeared to be idyllic when we first moved into my dream house in Chilolla Avenue. The situation seemed to deteriorate, however, from the day my engagement ring disappeared. The solitaire diamond ring was a substitute for the original, lost shortly after we were married. When replacing it we were, financially, in a much better position; hence it was not just a matter of being missed for sentimental value alone.

We had booked tickets to see a performance of *Godspell*, at the Little Theatre, the evening my ring went missing. When I had finished dressing I searched high and low for it; all to no avail. Eventually Ian's voice prompted me to get a move on. Not wishing to arrive late, I abandoned my quest and joined him without further delay.

The next day I summoned the houseboy and gardener, enlisting their help. Although we hunted inside and out, its whereabouts remained a complete mystery. However, I was beside myself with delight the following morning when John announced, with a hint of pride, that he had found it.

Overjoyed, I felt as if a great burden had been lifted from my shoulders.

'Where was it?' I demanded as I slipped the ring onto my finger, having examined it meticulously to ensure that it had in no way been damaged.

'I found it while I was sweeping the kitchen floor,' he replied, at the same time rubbing away an imaginary speck of grease from the cooker with his finger.

I knew instinctively that he was lying, as the night before I had scoured the area with a fine-tooth comb. Furthermore, I told him so in no uncertain terms.

Then the penny dropped. Could it be that John had discovered a lucrative sideline? I wondered.

Several months earlier he had approached me with the news that while removing leaves from the pool he had almost trodden on my watch which was lying in the grass. On that occasion I was exceedingly grateful and rewarded him generously.

Always willing to give others the benefit of the doubt, Ian pointed out that the houseboy might be covering up for someone else. 'For example, Soyashi could have taken it while playing in the house with Anthony and Fiona,' he pointed out. 'Mind you, if anything else disappears John and his family will have to go.'

The thought of finding a suitable replacement for the houseboy filled me with consternation. Consequently, on weighing up the pros and cons, I decided to take no further action. 'After all,' I reassured myself, 'without definite proof I could be judging him too harshly.'

The whole incident paled in comparison to the fate held in store for us the following Christmas. It was during a period when the state of the economy was deteriorating rapidly. Horrifying tales were on everybody's lips. No one felt safe at night as roving gangs robbed, attacked and sometimes murdered their unfortunate victims. It was rumoured that the ringleader was a white man. My gardener declared that on several occasions the man had been spotted by reliable witnesses but, rather like the Yeti, his identity remained a mystery.

It was not long before Ian felt compelled to hire security guards around the clock. By Christmas an alarm and floodlighting were in the process of being installed. We had been assured by the contractor that the latter would put Blackpool illuminations into the shade.

On the night disaster struck we decided to visit the Kitwe Club for a couple of hours. We knew the atmosphere would be convivial, as the festive season was already upon us. This certainly proved to be the case when we joined a lively bunch of friends we spotted propping up the bar. Armed with bottles of Coke and slices of biltong, the children made their way to the games room where a film was being shown; one of the popular Rocky numbers, I recall.

'That's a strange looking Father Christmas,' somebody commented jokingly, referring to Hugh Roberts as he made a beeline towards us. The cerise jacket he was wearing clashed painfully with the rest of his attire. The usually dapper gentleman appeared extremely dejected and acknowledged us with a nod only, before downing the whisky Ian placed in front of him.

'How's tricks?' I asked, only just remembering in time to decline the cigarette he offered me.

'Not good,' he retorted miserably, before relating in detail the events of the previous night, when his house had been burgled. 'They practically stole the clothes off my back while I was sleeping. I managed to borrow this outfit from a friend.'

This latest outrage triggered off a number of similar occurrences, to be related by a sympathetic audience only too willing to get in on the act.

I am not sure at which precise moment a feeling of uneasiness came over me, but, eventually, unable to relax and enjoy myself any longer, I decided to go home. Fortunately we had arrived in separate cars, so I was able to leave without putting an end to Ian's enjoyment.

Interrupting Hugh in mid-sentence I excused myself, at the same time abandoning an almost full glass of brandy. When I managed to prise Ian away from his colleagues, above the ear-splitting din, I informed him of my intentions, at the same time reminding him to keep an eye out for the children when their film came to an end.

'Will do, you worry too much,' he responded to my hasty peck on the cheek.

All appeared normal when I opened the front door and ran up the spiral stairway. However, having called the dogs repeatedly with no response whatsoever, I knew something must be drastically wrong. Turning on the light in the front room, I froze in my tracks as I regarded large empty gaps which had housed the television and stereo unit when we left home earlier that evening.

In horrified silence I contemplated the scene confronting me. It wasn't until the thought struck me that someone might still be lurking around the house that I pulled myself together and made for the telephone. 'Thank God!' I moaned when some minutes later the sound of car tyres crunching the chippings on the drive announced the arrival of Ian.

Together we made a complete tour of the building to discover the extent of the damage. The intruders had ransacked each room in turn. We gathered they must have been disturbed by my unexpected arrival, for several suitcases, crammed full of our belongings, lay abandoned on the children's beds. Their bedspreads, into which I imagined various items must have been bundled as the burglars made to leave, were nowhere to be seen.

Various books and irreplaceable photographs had been destroyed and strewn about the place. Ian bent to retrieve pieces of his driving licence, deliberately torn into shreds. The children must have felt devastated as they gazed at their possessions, damaged almost beyond recognition and discarded by unknown hands. In a corner of the front room the Christmas tree, decked out in all its sparkling finery, remained surprisingly unscathed.

From the state of the door it soon became apparent that the burglars, with the aid of an axe, had broken in through the poolside entrance to Fiona's bedroom. The rainy season had started with a vengeance that year, resulting in a soggy trail of discarded belongings, leading to a freshly made gap in the bougainvillaea hedge which bordered onto open bushland beyond.

Once we had recovered from the initial shock the question on all our lips was 'Where were the dogs?' Furthermore, what had happened to the guard? Without further ado, Ian made his way to the servants' quarters in order to investigate, leaving me to inform the police. Long before they arrived he had returned with the news that he had eventually found the guard and dogs. They were in the cellar, well out of harm's way, along with the houseboy and his family. When Ian had confronted the guard, John, coming to the terrified man's defence, had pleaded on his behalf. 'The dogs were barking at the gate, Bwana. Outside were some guys with guns. They tell Phiri, "Put dogs away and open gate or we will kill everyone." They then take all the keys and lock up everyone.'

When the police arrived just after midnight they carried out a thorough investigation, requesting a detailed list of all items stolen. To the best of our ability we wrote down what we considered to be missing, but months later were still discovering items inadvertently overlooked on the night. This included a couple of portable fans which we had found to be indispensable during the stifling summer months.

The officers then insisted upon interrogating the hapless guard and John, completely ignoring my protests when I considered they were becoming unnecessarily heavy-handed. Finally, unable to extract any further information, they advised us as a precaution to sack both the guard and the houseboy. We should then replace the dogs, for, as they so rightly pointed out, the animals might welcome rather than repel the servants should they return with vengeance in mind. Good advice we chose to ignore.

The next day we received a telephone call to say that the police had apprehended a couple of men carrying large bundles, the contents of which appeared to fit the description of some of the items on the list we had drawn up. When, shortly afterwards, Ian paid a visit to the station in order to identify our belongings, he was told to return in a couple of weeks' time should he wish to redeem them.

To my delight, one of the articles retrieved was a small bronze carriage clock which I cherished. My husband had presented it to me on our tenth wedding anniversary for – as he phrased it – putting up with him for a whole decade. Incredible at it may seem, a year or so later, it was stolen yet again. On that occasion the dogs alerted my husband who summoned the guard immediately. Close on the heels of the excited animals, they gave chase. Although the robbers escaped, fortunately for us, they were forced to discard most of their booty along the way. In the process, my little clock rolled under a bush at the bottom of the garden, where it was discovered by the children a few days later, none the worse for the experience.

The Van der Merwes had invited us over for drinks on Christmas morning, the day after the house had been ransacked. We had been looking forward to the occasion, but could not leave our home unattended until the damaged door had been secured and the security lights were functioning properly. When I telephoned Mia to cancel the invitation she was most sympathetic but adamant. 'You must drop off Fiona and Anthony; there's no reason why they should be penalised. Besides, Naomi and Giles will be perfect pests if they have no other children to play with.'

As we bundled the children into the car I agreed, at Ian's insistence, to stay at Mia's for a while. Admittedly, I needed little encouragement but, nevertheless, set out feeling slightly guilty at the thought of leaving my husband to celebrate on his own.

Upon our arrival I was handed a brandy by Marius, along with loads of sympathy from the other guests. As one drink led to another, I succeeded in drowning my sorrows and before long felt positively cheerful. When all the other guests had left, refusing 'one more for the road,' I persuaded Mia, Marius and family to share our Christmas dinner and continue the celebrations back at our place, in an endeavour to cheer up my housebound husband. Ian had been genuinely delighted when I telephoned to say there had been a change of plan.

As the overcrowded car drew up alongside the front door, he welcomed all with open arms. 'If Mohammed won't come to the mountain then hey presto,' Marius expressed theatrically as he alighted. During my absence Ian had surpassed himself, Christmas dinner being well under way. While the rest of us crowded around the bar, all the children volunteered to lay the table in order to demonstrate their artistic abilities. Everyone agreed that the combined effort was most praiseworthy. Having checked the turkey's excellent progress, I popped into the bedroom to freshen up. Before doing the necessary repairs, overcome by fatigue, I sat on the edge of the bed to catch my breath.

When I awoke, it was well past midnight. Feeling peckish, I made my way to the kitchen where I found Ian enjoying a final nightcap.

'Where is everyone?' I demanded petulantly.

'The Van der Merwes left ages ago, and the children went to bed shortly afterwards. Any moment now, I'm about to follow suit,' he stipulated, before draining an almost empty glass.

'What about the Christmas dinner?' I lamented, gazing at the mountain of dirty crockery, piled sky high on every available surface.

With a measure of pride in his voice he replied, 'Cooked to perfection.' Bidding me goodnight his parting words were, 'We tried to wake you but you were definitely out for the count.'

As I poked around the fridge for some left-overs, I suddenly remembered that we were holding open house in a few hours' time. Feeling like death warmed up I once more abandoned my husband and went in search of a 'hair of the dog'.

Although that particular Christmas could be described as being somewhat traumatic we nevertheless experienced some extremely enjoyable moments. I only wish I could add that our run of bad luck ended with the start of the New Year but, sadly, this was far from the case.

138

29

It was due to Vera Huxtable's efforts entirely that I became such an enthusiastic, if not outstanding, squash player.

On one of our trips to Livingstone Vera and her husband, Tim, having booked into the same hotel for a short break, had introduced themselves to us. After tolerating their company for the whole evening we came to the conclusion that, though well meaning, they were inclined to be somewhat supercilious.

Shortly after returning to the Copperbelt and whilst shopping at Parklands, I ran into Vera who greeted me like a long-lost friend. I groaned inwardly when she insisted that Ian and I dine at her place the following evening. At the same time, true to form, she let it slip that they would be entertaining several people of consequence. I searched desperately for a suitable reason why we would be unable to attend, but alas, at such short notice none was forthcoming.

When I mentioned my encounter with Vera to Ian, who normally welcomed any excuse for a get-together, he looked a trifle glum. 'I really should prefer it if you would not accept invitations on my behalf,' he reminded me plaintively.

It soon became evident that we had misjudged the Huxtables, for their virtues far outweighed any shortcomings. Due to their influence, we were accepted as members of the local Squash Racquets Club, where Vera spent hours teaching me the rudiments of the game. The full extent of her generosity was brought home to me when I overheard one of the other members mention that my friend's name was generally attached to one of the higher rungs of the competition ladder. Thinking I was well out of earshot, she then pointed out to her companion, 'Vera Huxtable will never reach the top playing with the likes of that one.'

The news that the Huxtables were abandoning their life on the Copperbelt came as a complete bombshell to a good many people. This, unfortunately, was the order of things to come, as one by one so many friends turned their backs on Zambia for pastures old and new.

Before leaving Tim and Vera decided to put most of their furniture and belongings up for auction. The occasion attracted people from far and wide as import licences for what the government considered to be luxuries were still more or less unobtainable. Consequently, most of the community relied solely on house sales when refurbishing their homes or replacing worn-out possessions.

Figoff, an auctioneer of some repute, was already dancing attendance when we arrived at the Huxtables. Several attractive pieces had caught our attention the previous evening, during a tour of inspection; consequently, we were anxious for the bidding to start.

The children were delighted when Ian's bid for the last of several job lots remained unchallenged. Later, amongst a plethora of toys, games and puzzles we discovered a nearly new croquet set. Once installed on our front lawn, it took everyone's fancy and we spent many a happy hour challenging each other and many a willing visitor to a game.

A close friend and teacher had recently pointed out that it was high time my children were given the opportunity to enrich their lives through learning to play a musical instrument. Unfortunately, my bid for lot no. nineteen, an old upright piano, fell far short of the reserve limit.

Refusing to feel defeated, I arranged for the children to receive piano lessons and advertised far and wide for a suitable instrument. Eventually, my efforts were rewarded. Ellis, one of my swimming pupils and the son of an American evangelical minister, informed me that the piano in his father's church hall was shortly to be replaced. 'Just call me Nathan,' his father had volunteered when I addressed him as Reverend Bianchi while arranging an appointment over the telephone.

Admittedly, I was inclined to be a little apprehensive about meeting Nathan at the church hall on my own. I had recently discovered that his son had a tendency to relate jokes and stories of a dubious nature. This he generally chose to do at the most inopportune moment. When showing my disapproval, Ellis had insisted that his father regularly entertained the family with such vulgar titbits at supper time. It appeared that 'the family' had been generously extended

140

to include several fellow citizens who shared a similar religious philosophy.

As it turned out my doubts were groundless, for when I introduced myself to Nathan, his mind was on a far higher plane. Before discussing the purpose of my visit, he subjected me to a thorough tour of the establishment, accompanied by a running religious commentary.

Whilst standing on a large stage at the front of the hall my concentration wavered as I peered down at a small pool built into the foundations. In way of an explanation the preacher proffered, 'That's our baptismal font, into which all new recruits are immersed completely naked.'

'Oh! I've already been baptised,' I assured him hastily, not wishing to be considered in the least bit eligible. For a moment he seemed to be slightly bewildered and concentrated on the receptacle below. Then, without warning, he flung back his head and, literally, shook with laughter. Attempting to join in the hilarity I could not help wondering if the incident, considerably embellished, would later become a topic of frivolity for the supper table, much to the delight of his son Ellis.

On a more sober note we then progressed to the subject of the piano. 'Over the years, the old piano has served the Lord well,' Nathan commented, as if that in itself was sufficient recommendation. Less than impressed, I brought to his attention the fact that, apart from a complete overhaul, several parts would need to be replaced. At this the minister promised to give me the name of someone, who, he assured me, could handle any such problem.

Several years later, when my own precious possessions fell under the hammer, I received more than twice the amount negotiated that day in the church hall. At the time, however, aware it was a vendor's market, I thought I was paying well over the odds for something that could have been well beyond redemption!

We installed the piano in a corner of the dining room. Here, we hoped, the children would be able to practise without disturbing the rest of the household beyond endurance. I managed to contact Jackson Kapikila, the piano tuner recommended by Reverend Bianchi. In time, he managed to renovate our instrument if not restore it to its former glory.

141

Some time later John announced one morning that there was someone at the gate asking if we had any furniture in need of repair. As it so happened, there were several items around the house requiring attention. The man claimed to be a carpenter and French polisher by trade. He introduced himself as Joseph, but was so advanced in years that we usually referred to him as Madalla – old man – out of respect. Pleased with the results of his labour, we next commissioned him to re-polish the piano and several other articles.

I eventually became quite attached to the old man, going out of my way to keep him employed. While he worked he would go to great lengths to explain each stage and why he used certain ingredients, almost as if I were his apprentice.

When the children left Lechwe Primary School to continue their education down south, I asked Sylvia, their music teacher, if she would consider accepting me as a substitute. Although initially reluctant to do so, she eventually caved in under my persistent pleas.

I had enjoyed learning to play the piano as a child but, unfortunately, upon reaching puberty, had abandoned the instrument. Instead I concentrated on ballet lessons, filled with impossible fantasies of some day replacing Fonteyn, the irreplaceable. Under Sylvia's excellent guidance, however, I soon made up for those lost years. Regrettably, subsequent reports from successive music teachers eventually convinced me that the children had not been endowed with the same tenacity.

The day of the auction did not come to a close completely without drama, due entirely to carelessness on my part. Forgetting the guard had asked for time off to attend a funeral that day, I had not requested a replacement. To make matters worse, upon our return Ian had warned me to be sure to lock the gates properly. In my impatience to examine our newly-acquired possessions, I failed to do so.

Later, when John went off duty, he returned almost immediately with a look of consternation written all over his face. 'Madam come quick, Kim has bitten a madonna,' he informed me woefully. It was then I remembered the guard and groaned inwardly. Going to investigate, I was dismayed to discover that the dog had bitten the back of an old woman's leg quite badly. It transpired that while looking for work she had banged on our front gates with a metal implement, hoping to attract attention. Growing impatient, she had proceded to rattle the gates, causing them to swing apart. The outraged dog, grasping the opportunity on all fours, had immediately attacked the intruder.

After John and I had rendered first aid, Ian took over and drove the unfortunate woman to hospital, where she was given the necessary treatment. After arranging to compensate her generously he drove her to her compound, hoping she would put the whole unpleasant incident behind her.

No such luck, however, for the following evening around dusk, whilst sitting on the balcony, I was to witness the arrival of a large dilapidated vehicle from which four burly men alighted. Intercepted by my husband, they started to gesticulate with voices raised. Although I could not hear what was being said, it was fairly obvious that something was amiss. I could not believe that the guard would have, willingly, permitted such unsavoury characters to enter our front gates. With this in mind I went in search of Ian's recently acquired gas gun which he kept under our mattress. It had been purchased with the intention of being used as a deterrent, rather than a lethal weapon which, I understood, it was not. Nevertheless, having seen the previous owner use it to disperse a bunch of stray dogs, I knew it could be extremely effective. Retrieving the weapon, I covered it with a tea towel before joining Ian in the garden.

As I approached my husband, however, the intruders dismissed themselves, returning to their vehicle. As we watched them drive away, Ian, outraged, explained the purpose of their visit. They had arrived with the intention of persuading him, gently or otherwise, to increase the amount of compensation he had given the old madonna. 'At first I told them to get lost,' he exploded with indignation. 'When, however, they threatened to report the incident to the police, pointing out that the dog had broken the law and would have to be destroyed, I relented. After all the poor creature was only doing its duty. Finally I agreed to arrange and pay for the woman to attend a private clinic for further treatment and checkups. Still not satisfied, they then insisted I also cover the cost of a taxi to collect her from and return her to her home, before and after each visit.'

At first, I felt extremely guilty about the whole business as I knew I was solely to blame. Any feeling of remorse, however, soon gave way to one of indignation. Having related in detail how I had attempted to come to the rescue with the aid of his gas gun, instead of being complemented for showing courage and initiative, my husband seemed capable of appreciating only the humorous side of the situation.

30

For several months we made a concerted effort to find suitable preparatory schools for Anthony and Fiona to attend, when they finished their primary education at Lechwe. After weighing all the pros and cons we decided to apply to St Andrews College and the sister school, Diocesan School for Girls, both situated in Grahamstown, South Africa. Once the children knew they had been accepted they wanted to start immediately. Anthony transferred to St Andrews the following January, when he was ten. Fiona, his junior by fourteen months, commenced her education at DSG eighteen months later.

Much to the envy of our friends, Ian managed the almost impossible by acquiring a couple of tickets to travel on the Blue Train from Cape Town to Johannesburg. The date stamped on the voucher suited our purpose admirably for we would be taking Fiona to start her new school around that time. If everything went according to plan, on the return journey we would be able to travel part of the way by Blue Train.

During Fiona's last term at Lechwe, we decided to celebrate her birthday by spending a long weekend in Kariba. It meant we would miss the Independence Day celebrations, which hardly mattered for at the time there appeared to be little for anyone to celebrate. Anthony would be unable to join us as he was spending half-term with Uncle Ian and his family at Harveya; a great treat.

My husband, unfortunately, developed a high temperature on the journey and when we arrived at the Cutty Sark, spent most of the weekend resting in our hotel bedroom. Fiona and I filled our days relaxing by the pool or driving around the delightful holiday resort, enjoying wonderful views from Kariba Heights or browsing around the few general stores. Although Ian made an effort to join us for dinner in the evenings, he could eat little and wilted visibly.

By the time December arrived he was still suffering from what we believed to be the unpleasant after-effects of a bout of influenza.

Somewhat concerned about the state of his health, I persuaded him to book a fortnight's holiday in Durban when the children broke up for the Christmas holidays.

We met Anthony's plane from Port Elizabeth as it landed at Jan Smuts. Nicknamed the Lollipop Express it was chock-a-block with pupils from the various schools and colleges in Grahamstown. Our son couldn't wait to acquaint us 'bush bunnies' with the customs of his new academic world. In retaliation, we pointed out that he had picked up a 'yarpy' accent.

Early the following morning, collecting a hire car, we journeyed across acres of open plains and rolling hills, eventually arriving at Newcastle, where we intended to spend the night. During the drive we broke our journey outside Volksrust and made for Amajuba – The Hill of Doves – where at O'Neill's cottage, in 1881, a treaty was signed between the British and the Boers to end the First War of Independence.

Next morning, after a good night's rest at the Holiday Inn we continued our journey south. Passing through Dundee we made for Buffalo River to capture some of the atmosphere of the fierce battle fought in 1879 at Rorke's Drift. Deep in contemplation, one scene in particular from the film *Zulu* came flooding back to me. A friend had brought the film around one night and we had watched it after dinner. One small incident which took place during the performance brought a smile to everyone's lips. It happened during a scene when 130 Redcoats attempt to ward off an attack by an endless sea of Zulus who appeared over the ridge of a hill. Menacingly, the warriors advance towards the British stronghold, to the unnerving rhythm of pounding feet – a thoroughly awesome sight.

My then eight-year-old, who had been sitting on the floor a few feet in front of the rest of us, rose cautiously. As the imposing rows of warriors advanced step by step towards the front of the screen, so Anthony retreated in similar fashion. Lowering himself onto Ian's knee, he clasped his father's hand for reassurance, but not for one instant did his eyes leave the screen.

Before leaving the site of that great battle we visited the Swedish Mission station established in 1876, and extended during the 1960s to include a tribal arts and crafts centre. Various items of handwoven articles, wood sculptures and pottery were for sale. I bought a small, grey sandstone elephant, but accidentally broke it before reaching Durban.

Time permitted only a fleeting tour of Ladysmith. During the Second War of Independence of 1899-1902, troops and British residents of the town were besieged by the Boers for 115 days. Guidebook in hand we entered the Anglican church of All Saints, where we reflected upon the stained glass windows and memorial tablets inscribed with the names of over 3000 British soldiers who lost their lives defending the town of Ladysmith.

As time ran out, unable to visit other places of interest associated with the siege, we had to content ourselves with the promise of a second chance sometime in the future. Bypassing Pietermaritzburg, noteworthy for its Voortrekker homes and colonial buildings, we continued along the last leg of our journey.

At Kerkenberg an elderly Afrikaner with little knowledge of the English language pointed us in the direction of Retiefklip. Now a tourist attraction, its claim to fame is a rock upon which Voortrekker leader Piet Retief's daughter, Debra, painted his name and date of his fifty-seventh birthday – 12th November, 1837.

Shrouded in the past, we made a detour through Botha's Hill and Drummond, to be rewarded with magnificent views of the Valley of a Thousand Hills. Rejoining the N3 at Hillcrest, we made a steady descent into Durban. Leaving the Western Freeway, we motored along Marine to South Beach. On the front, outside the Aquarium, decorated rickshaws drawn by brightly dressed Zulus for a few moments distracted our attention from the inviting waters of the Indian Ocean.

Our stay in Durban turned into a nightmare as Ian's usual boundless energy and enthusiasm deserted him completely. Deciding to take it at an easy pace, we spent the first week on and around South Beach, within a stone's throw of our hotel. Numerous restaurants, ice cream parlours and a range of various sporting facilities saved us from having to search further afield for entertainment. Nevertheless, after lunch one afternoon, we took a short drive up the coast to Umhalnga Rocks. The trip proved well worth while as we spent several enjoyable hours exploring this unspoilt, prestigious seaside resort.

At one point I recall stopping to look around one of the sleepy little stores which we encountered along the way. Intent on buying a sun hat, I proceeded to try on several of various shapes and sizes. Before long Ian and the children followed suit. This caused a good deal of hilarity but I don't suppose the shopkeeper felt at all amused especially as, somewhat sheepishly, we left empty-handed.

During dinner that evening Ian literally picked at his meal, hardly able to eat a morsel. He really didn't look at all well and admitted to feeling exhausted. The following morning I persuaded him to see a doctor, recommended by the hotel receptionist, who managed to arrange an appointment for that afternoon. The outcome was that Ian was advised to consult a specialist without further delay. While Ian spent the best part of the following day as an outpatient in a clinic in Durban, I entertained the children to the best of my ability, trying not to burden them with my anxieties.

With street guide in hand, we explored a little on foot. Cutting across West and Smith, we made for the Victoria Embankment overlooking the Bay of Natal. Pausing for a while, I stopped to admire the baroque Da Gama Clock. It had been presented to the city by the Portuguese Government in 1897 to commemorate the discovery of Port Natal by Vasco Da Gama in 1497. The children were far more interested, however, in the Dick King memorial, further along the embankment. Bombarded with questions, I turned once more to my National Tourists' Guide for assistance. The statue had been erected in honour of Dick King and his Zulu companion, Ndongeni, who rode the 960 kilometres to Grahamstown in just ten days in order to secure reinforcements for the beleaguered British troops in Durban.

Tired of sightseeing, we made our way to the beach for a swim. Once there, we spotted a sign warning swimmers to watch out for 'Bluebottles.' Mystified we approached the lifeguard who informed us that this was a type of jellyfish with a nasty sting. Deciding not to tempt fate further, I encouraged the children to take advantage of the trampolines situated further along the beach. Before returning to the hotel we played pitch and putt for a while, always a great favourite.

Ian returned to the hotel later that evening with news that was far from reassuring. The consultant had advised him to cut short his vacation and return to Johannesburg for further tests. With a heavy heart I packed that night in preparation for an early start the following morning.

148

A couple of days later, around noon, we checked into the Johannesburg Airport Holiday Inn. After a quick brush up we made our way to the coffee bar for lunch. When coffee was served the children went outside to play on the swings. From a table by the window we were able to keep an eye on them while we discussed future plans until it was time for Ian to leave for the clinic.

The following day the children and I seemed to spend hours in front of the television set in our hotel room. I must have watched nearly every programme scheduled, but registered nothing. Around six o'clock that evening I received a message from the clinic to say that the surgeon dealing with my husband's case had decided to perform a biopsy. As it transpired, my husband was not discharged until the following evening, for the operation had not gone as smoothly as expected. When Ian finally arrived back at the hotel, just before midnight, I was shocked by his appearance and fought with determination to put on a brave face.

31

Towards the middle of January Anthony returned to Grahamstown and Fiona, whose days at Lechwe were drawing to a close, could not wait to join him. Ian and I were impatient for that all-important telephone call from Johannesburg, confirming the results of Ian's tests, and finally putting an end to all speculation.

I was busy in the kitchen when the call came through. Several minutes later Ian appeared in the doorway. From the expression on his face I gathered all was not well. Although our holiday in Durban may not have been a resounding success, once we returned home Ian's health seemed to improve by leaps and bounds, convincing me that there could be nothing seriously wrong with him.

He had a malignant tumour. For the next few weeks, still dazed by this disclosure, I would recall snippets of conversation which, in the past, I had overheard by those who had found themselves to be in a similar situation. 'They do wonders nowadays,' I would reassure myself time after time. With a glimmer of hope the thought passed through my mind that the consultant could well have given Ian someone else's results in error, but this proved to be cold comfort.

Ian, ever hopeful, became a willing guinea pig for any new drug on the market and, when these failed to halt the malignant growth, received more than his fair share of radium. Eventually it was the cure rather than the disease that proved to be his downfall. In the meantime, between trips to Johannesburg for treatment, we slipped bit by bit back into our once familiar routine and started to enjoy life again, if not with quite the same exuberance.

Without a doubt we had our bad days. For example there was the time we discovered that my husband's hair was falling out in handfuls. A spurned bush hat came to the rescue on that occasion. Then, during a visit to the golf club, one of the committee members unwittingly instructed Ian to remove his headgear in the confines of the clubhouse. When my husband chose to ignore his demands the man, with displeasure, aired his views in public, much to the embarrassment of those who were aware of Ian's predicament.

However, it was not all gloom and doom – we even had our humorous moments! I can remember using a magnifying glass to take a closer look at Ian's completely bald crown, while reassuring him that the new growth would soon be visible to the naked eye. This was no empty promise for, in time, he once more possessed a fine head of thick dark hair.

It wasn't until some time later that Ian admitted to me that, during a brief visit to London for a second opinion, a Harley Street specialist had confirmed the original prognosis. During the appointment he informed my husband that according to the law of averages, Ian had approximately two years in which to sort out his affairs. Upon his return, preferring to keep me in blissful ignorance, Ian assured me that the specialist had seemed pleased with his progress. Wanting to believe this was indeed the case, I left it at that and probed no further.

At last the time arrived for Fiona to spread her wings and accompany her brother when he returned to Grahamstown. 'Becoming a boarder makes you feel important – like Anthony,' she confided in earnest.

At that time there was no direct flight from the Copperbelt to South Africa. The least complex route involved travelling to Malawi in order to catch a connection from Blantyre to Johannesburg. Arriving at Jan Smuts Airport just after sundown, we spent the night at the now familiar airport Holiday Inn. Next morning we boarded a plane to Port Elizabeth, where we had stopped for a break when touring the Garden Route some years earlier. The children were delighted that we planned a brief visit to the resort before driving on to Grahamstown.

Anthony and Fiona soon lost all track of time as they bathed in the rolling surf at Kings Beach, disputing whether next to have a round on the putt-putt course or display their skills on the trampolines. Another favourite attraction was the giant open-air chess board at Happy Valley. Though late in the season, the children clamoured to climb aboard the Apple Express. This much admired narrow gauge steam train runs between Port Elizabeth and Aventuur, passing through enchanting orchards in the Langhloof Valley.

151

On our last day we succeeded in climbing the 204-step staircase of the campanile, erected to commemorate the landing of the 1820 settlers. Our efforts were well rewarded with a panoramic view of Port Elizabeth's impressive harbour, to the sound of a carillon of twenty-three bells ringing the changes.

Each glorious hour flew by and before we knew it the day arrived for us to continue our journey. Reaching Grahamstown, Anthony was eager to point out various places of distinction. Focusing on the cathedral, my son pronounced with a look of delight, 'That is the best church I have ever been to.' Amazed we begged him to reveal all. 'The vicar throws sweets to us after the service,' he disclosed. The prime attraction, however, was a certain burger bar in the town centre, to which all 'preppies' escaped whenever possible. This occasion proved to be no exception; it was crowded to bursting point with returning schoolfellows.

Appetites satisfied, tummies bulging, we prised the children away from their idea of paradise with a view to paying a visit to the new 1820 Settlers' Monument on Gunfire Hill. This imposing structure, comprising a theatre, auditorium and conference centre, seemed far removed from the days when wagonloads of pioneers had to take refuge from the marauding Xhosa.

Outside the entrance we posed to have our photo taken by an obliging member of staff who then suggested, should time permit, that we make our way to Makana Handicrafts at number eight Bathurst Street. Taking his advice, we found a convenient spot to park before wandering around the showrooms, where exquisitely handwoven wall-hangings and carpets, priced a trifle beyond my pocket, were on display.

Driving past Rhodes University, I felt duty bound to take a quick look at some of the exhibits in the Albany and Settlers' Memorial Museums, situated on campus. The children, however, were less than enthusiastic. Instead we agreed unanimously to return to the burger bar for further refreshment. Looking back, we seemed to have crammed an awful lot into just one day.

Before saying goodbye to Fiona, we did a quick tour of her new school. Remembering, with mixed feelings, my own experiences as a boarder, I was pleasantly surprised by the relaxed and happy atmosphere that prevailed. When it was time for us to leave, waving madly until our small daughter disappeared from view, we drove on to St Andrews.

We parted from our son at the front entrance, where several boys from his house were already unloading their belongings. Although both the children had attempted to put on a brave face, it turned out to be a heartrending experience. Furthermore, the promise of a first class education, failed dismally, at the time, to compensate for the separation.

32

'Remember it's the quality rather than the quantity of life that is important,' the Dutchman had remarked on an occasion when I was feeling particularly down. How often I was to reflect upon his words during the following months!

From the moment our plane touched down in the Cape, however, our days were filled with wonderment, leaving little time for either Ian or myself to dwell on what the future might hold in store.

We hired a car at D.F. Malan Airport, and drove straight to our hotel overlooking the bay. Towering above this fairest of capes, Table Mountain provided an exquisite backdrop.

That afternoon, after consulting a map of the area, we set out for the town centre. Along Eastern Boulevard, joining the Kloof Nek Road, we made for View Point at Signal Hill. From this lofty height we were richly rewarded with an incredible view over Cape Town. As darkness fell the twinkling city made a compelling sight.

There seemed so much to fit into the next few days, so we decided to explore a few of the galleries and museums we had missed out on previous visits. Most days, aiming for the town centre, we managed to park the car just off the Strand. From there we were in walking distance of a number of the locations we intended visiting during our brief stay.

Crossing Adderley, we reached Koopmans-De Wet House, situated on the corner of Strand and Long Street. Now a national monument, parts of which date back to 1701, members of the De Wet family lived there for over a hundred years. As I feasted my eyes on what had once been some of their priceless possessions, with a certain amount of envy I pictured the lifestyle they would have led in those far-off days. Outside in the quadrangle we stumbled across a 200-year-old grapevine which still, so we were told, bears fruit in season.

We had no difficulty in finding the Cultural History Museum situated in Adderley Street. Originally the Slave Lodge of the Dutch East Indian Company, in 1679, it served as the First Supreme Court in 1809. As a museum, it boasts a rare collection of early Cape furniture, ladies' fashions, coins and stamps, along with a replica of a vintage chemist shop.

In the cobbled courtyard the remains of the founder of the settlement at the Cape, Jan Van Riebeeck, and his wife, Maria, had been laid to rest. Earlier, at the upper end of Heerengracht we had encountered bronze statues standing side by side, erected in their memory.

We usually returned to the hotel around dusk. Battling against strong breezes, we would make our way from the car-park up a steep incline, leading to the foyer. After repairing the day's damage, I would then join Ian in the lounge bar where we relaxed for a while before changing for dinner.

One morning we parked near the Harbour Cafe and took the Penny ferry to the Clock Tower. Having failed to check first, we were disappointed to discover it was closed to the public on that occasion. This did not prevent us from enjoying the rest of the trip, however, which consisted of a tour of the Victoria Basin in the old part of Table Bay Harbour. Basking in the sunshine, we sailed past a variety of commercial vessels, tugs and boats of the deep-sea fishing fleet.

Another day we went in search of the Castle. Dating back to 1666, it was built in the shape of a five-pointed star by Van Riebeeck and successive governors of the Dutch East Indian Company. During a guided tour of the dungeons we were given a list of numerous gory details, best forgotten.

Visiting the Maritime Museum, we inspected various interesting models of ships and other relics. An equally fine array of uniforms and weaponry was also on display at the Military Museum. Climbing a short flight of steps leading onto the Kat Balcony, we entered exquisitely furnished State Rooms. Here my imagination once more ran riot as I admired a prized collection of paintings and furnishings of times long gone.

Having had more than our fair share of culture, we then wandered aimlessly between the stalls at the sweet-smelling flower market in Trafalgar Place, listening to the flower sellers as they chatted extravagantly in a mixture of Afrikaans and some unknown dialect.

The Botanic Gardens off Government Avenue proved to be

155

another rewarding diversion. The site, today, is covered in an abundance of flowers, trees, rose gardens and hot houses – all magnificent. Once it had been the vegetable garden of Jan Van Riebeeck, established with the intention of growing fresh produce for passing ships. We rounded off a perfect afternoon by visiting the open-air tea garden where refreshments were served under the scrutiny of an abundance of doves and inquisitive squirrels.

For me the best was yet to come. On our last day we set out in the direction of Cape Point. Looking back at Table Mountain, I remembered with nostalgia the cable ride we had taken to the summit on our first visit, some years earlier. Casting my mind back in time, I recalled that a thick vaporous blanket had covered Cape Town that morning. Rising above the clouds, we experienced an awe-inspiring vista as Devil's Peak and the Lion's Head emerged precipitously out of a billowy vale of mist.

I can remember leaving the cableway to stroll along the 'Table Top' as far as Platteslip Gorge. Further on we came to Echo Valley where, with lungs fully expanded, our voices reverberated across the plateau. Eventually, arriving at the highest point, Maclear's Beacon, we were rewarded with truly magnificent views. Amongst the flora growing close by we had uncovered glacial scarred pebbles recording the eclipse of an ancient Ice Age.

Before returning to the cable car we visited The Tearoom close by. Over a piping hot cup of tea, I wrote several promised postcards which I then popped into a postbox outside. During the descent, I was impressed to learn that all correspondence posted from there would bear the postmark 'Table Mountain'.

During that holiday we became acquainted with an ancient legend, which took place at Saddle Rock, connecting Devil's Peak to the Mountain. It went something like this: a retired pirate named Van Hunks, out climbing one day, encountered the devil. For a while the two of them smoked their pipes, chatting amicably. As Van Hunks was preparing to move on, his smoking companion informed the pirate that, for his sins, he had earned himself a place in Hell. Before departing, by staking his soul, Van Hunks, persuaded the devil to join him in a smoking contest. It is claimed that the competition is still in progress to this very day. It takes place only during the summer months, however, as due to their advanced years, the pair no longer care to venture onto the mountain when the weather is inclement.

I was immediately brought back to reality as Ian handed me a route map of the Peninsula. Taking the M6, we drove south to Hout Bay – so named on account of the area having provided timber for the masts of ships belonging to the East India Company. If time had permitted, from the harbour we could have taken a short boat ride to Duiker Island, noted for seals and a variety of bird life. Instead, adding yet another name to our list of next time musts, we feasted on crayfish washed down with delicious, locally produced wine.

From Hout Bay we travelled along the coastal road known as Chapman's Drive, renowned for mile upon mile of unrivalled scenery. Exhilarated, we gazed upon a breathtaking vista, challenged by the sea over 150 metres below on one side, and 300 metres of sheer rock on the other. From Chapman's Point the M6 drove us inland in the direction of Kommetjie. A cold blustery wind kept the temperature at bay as we passed small towns and estuaries, some with the most odd-sounding names such as Noorhoek, Scarborough and Smitswinkel. Outside a small store a colourful sign advertising freshly ground hot coffee proved too much of a temptation. Once inside the shop I ordered two black coffees without sugar to which the proprietor commented, 'Ah! A true connoisseur.' Smiling politely, I failed to reveal the bottle of sweeteners concealed in my pocket.

Referring once again to our well-worn *Guide Map for Tourists*, we learned that the Cape of Good Hope Nature Reserve was established in 1939 to preserve the scenic beauty, fauna and flora of the Cape Peninsula. This we could not dispute. The herds of black wildebeest, baboon and various bok known to inhabit the region, however, seemed a bit thin on the ground that particular day.

Approaching Cape Point, we ran out of tarmac and parked the car on a dirt track a short distance from the sea. Drawn by the sound of waves crashing against the rocks, I hurriedly followed a well-worn trail. Reaching the shore, I bent down and ran my fingers through the invigorating, icy cold waters of the Atlantic Ocean.

A mini bus named the Flying Dutchman carried us to the top of the peak. Climbing a flight of steps, we came across the site of Old Cape Point lighthouse. Here we rested for a while against a rocky outcrop, delighting in the breathtaking, panoramic views of the Cape of Good Hope and False Bay in the distance.

Later, when stopping to examine a monument commemorating Portuguese navigators who had pioneered the sea route round the Cape of Good Hope, a notice caught my eye. It stated quite simply, 'Take nothing but photos – leave nothing but footprints.'

Returning to the car, reluctant to depart immediately, we turned on the radio. For a while we listened to part of a recording of Beethoven's Fifth Piano Concerto, being performed by the Cape Town Symphony Orchestra. As the ethereal strains of the adagio faded, I was filled with a certain poignancy. Silently I recalled the Dutchman's words relating to the quality of life. As if reading my thoughts, Ian remarked spontaneously, 'Lekker man.'

There were still plenty of surprises in store, during our return trip to Cape Town, that glorious day. Simonstown, noteworthy for its Historical Mile of ancient buildings, encouraged us to delay longer than necessary. At one point not far from the naval base, our car was forced to a halt for the firing of a cannon. Although I recall being startled by the sudden explosion, the significance of the occasion now, unfortunately, escapes me.

Stopping for a while at Kalk Bay, we visited the breakwater where, overshadowed by cavernous mountains, anglers, lines cast in hope, waited patiently. Ignoring the temptation to stay and explore, we drove on through St James, stopping at the cottage where Rhodes died in 1902. Browsing around his personal relics, I remembered the time, when passing through the Matopos outside Bulawayo, we had travelled to the Top of the World. Deeply moved, I had gazed upon the grave of this truly great man laid to rest surrounded by a sombre landscape of boulders.

Darkness was fast approaching by the time we reached Muizenberg Beech. Joining the Simon Van Der Stel Freeway, we bypassed Groot Constantia where, on a previous occasion, we had admired the Cape Dutch architecture while visiting a museum housing antique furniture, glassware and porcelain.

In the shadowy darkness, we drove past Rhodes Memorial and the Groote Shuur Hospital where, fifteen years earlier, Professor C. Barnard had performed the first heart transplant.

Shortly after returning to our hotel, we booked a call to

Grahamstown, having promised to contact the children before departing from the Cape. No longer so homesick, they appeared to be in high spirits. This was due to the fact that Uncle Ian, who had once been a pupil at St Andrews, had promised to take them to Kenton-on-Sea for a short half-term break. This was a real treat, as they would be staying at his cottage close to the seafront. There they would be encouraged to canter along the beach on horseback during the hours of daylight and chase hares by the light of the moon.

On our last night in the Cape, before falling asleep, I looked back with great pleasure on what had been such a happy time. Although I yearned to stay, this did not prevent me from speculating about the many delights which lay ahead, the following day, aboard the Blue Train.

33

At last, the day we had been waiting for arrived. It was Sunday, 30th January, 1983. Arriving at Cape Town railway station in good time, we were given a cordial welcome and shown to our compartment aboard the Blue Train. I was immediately impressed by the luxurious furniture, fittings and rich golden colour scheme. Glancing around I noticed, adorning one of the walls, an attractive reproduction by Pierneef, a South African artist of some renown.

Our attendant explained that a minute layer of gold had been diffused into one side of the window in order to deflect heat and glare. He added that any photographs taken through this type of glass would have an attractive rosy glow. Putting this to the test some time later, we were delighted with the results.

Pointing to the control console beneath the window, he then demonstrated that, with the flick of a switch, one could select music, alter the temperature, open or close the Venetian blinds and summon a member of staff. He also mentioned that a shoe-cleaning service was available. 'Just place your shoes in the built-in cabinet, over there on the corridor side of the compartment. In due course, they will be removed, polished and returned to the locker, from an opening on the outside.'

It was also brought to our attention that a slim-necked tap on the wash basin provided a never-ending supply of ice cold drinking water, throughout the trip. This proved to be no major attraction at that precise moment, for our attention kept returning to the bottle of champagne, placed beside two crystal flutes on a small table, compliments of the railway company.

As the hour of departure approached we stepped into the corridor, built on the scenic side of the route, in order to keep the heat of the sun away from the accommodation area.

At 9.00 a.m. precisely the Blue Train's diesel engines came to life as our hotel on wheels glided noiselessly out of the station. Slowly gaining speed, we were soon travelling along at a dignified forty miles per hour. Taking one last lingering look, I was sadly aware that we were swiftly abandoning the magic of the Cape forever.

Returning to our compartment, twisting the serrated knob below the door handle, for a while, we sipped champagne and participated in whatever else might have taken our fancy, at that time, in the privacy of such luxurious surroundings.

Later, deciding to explore a little, we made our way to the lounge car, dominated by an afromosia timber ceiling. Full length, finger pleated curtains blended in with the rest of the autumn gold decor. Plushly upholstered armchairs rested upon wall to wall carpeting of the thickest pile. Once again, one was tempted to admire the mastery of Pierneef, placed strategically around the room. A bar and matching stools, padded in soft creamy leather, caught our attention. At the same time a smiling attendant greeted us pleasantly. Amongst the wide range of wines and beverages he had on display were several eye-catching souvenirs. As a memento of our fascinating journey, Ian bought a white beer tankard with the words 'The Blue Train', and the company's emblem embellished in gold.

Around noon, we went to lunch. Exquisitely engraved doors stood at each entrance to the dining car. Halfway down the coach, situated between stately timber table dividers, a floral display of some of South Africa's loveliest flowers was a sight to behold.

The catering department seemed to have surpassed themselves, offering, amongst various other culinary delights, kingclip mornay, fresh salmon with mayonnaise, and fillet of beef richelieu. After a more than generous helping of rainbow trifle for dessert, I was obliged to forego a tantalising assortment of cheese and biscuits.

Sipping my coffee, I noticed that particular attention had been paid to the design of the menu which was printed in black on a plain white background. The company's emblem, and two small bunches of protea, were depicted in gold, the latter enriched with touches of green, pink and orange.

After lunch we returned to the lounge car, where my copy of the latest paperback failed to compete with the magnificent scenery for any length of time.

The dining car took on a much more romantic mood in the evening. Under subdued lighting we dined upon crayfish and rib of beef cooked to perfection. Though tempted by the chocolate and cherry pudding, I turned to the cheese board which proved to be a delicious alternative. Needless to say, an excellent selection of South African wines to suit the most discriminating of palates was available.

After dinner, no longer able to admire the outside world go flashing by, we returned to the lounge car. Enjoying a nightcap, we chatted amicably to some of our fellow travellers. Those out of touch with life beyond the Limpopo questioned us closely. It appeared that most of their compatriots who had strayed so far north had returned home soon after independence was granted to Zambia in 1964.

For most of the journey we derived much pleasure from plotting our journey with the help of the route guide, distributed by South African Railways. Leafing through the pages, we picked up various bits of interesting information as we covered the 1432 kilometres from Cape Town to Johannesburg.

Once under way, gaining speed, the line of rail headed for Belleville. Originally known as Twelve Mile Stone or the Durban Road, today it is an important rail junction. Some miles to the east lay Stellenbosch nestling in the Eerste River Valley. With eyes cast in that direction, I recalled Van der Stel's legacy of oak trees in Dorp Street, with tops entwined to form a shady arbour. Having lost none of its old world charm, Stellenbosch is still considered to be the gem of the Cape.

From the train we spotted Taalmonument – the Language Monument, inaugurated in 1975, to symbolise the Afrikaans language.

To Paarl I will some day return. Sprawling along the banks of the Berg River, the town derives its name from the three massive granite boulders which tower aloft, glistening like pearls in the sunlight after a shower of rain.

In season the tips of the snow-capped Drakenstein Mountains create a magnificent backdrop. Voraciously, we feasted our eyes on the steep lower slopes, still covered with summer's green foliage of grapevine, contrasting picturesquely with the bleak gradients above. Descendents of the French Huguenots, who settled in the region in 1688, are still reputed to produce the best wine in South Africa.

De Doorns, named after the thorn bushes which abounded when it

162

was discovered in 1709, is now surrounded by vineyards and orchards. The pastel hues of surrounding mountain peaks change ethereally, according to the time of day. From here we bade farewell to the picturesque vine-covered valleys of the Cape. It is alleged their kaleidoscopic seasons were responsible for delaying trekkers journeying north to the plains, koppies and scrubland of the less fertile Karoo.

Journeying on we slipped past what had once been known as Montagu Road, enigmatically renamed Touws River in 1883. Perhaps a clue lies in the Hottentot word Touws, meaning 'port' or 'gate'.

Waiting for the engine to be changed at Beaufort West, we alighted and walked along the platform to take a closer look. Chatting to some of the crew, we learnt that the power car – the heart of the Blue Train – is capable of supplying sufficient energy to light a medium-sized town. An anti-skid device controls the doors which are automatically locked once the train exceeds eight kilometres an hour. We also learned that the train is normally hauled between Cape Town and Johannesburg by electric generators. On the section between Kimberley and Beaufort West diesel locomotives are generally put to use. However, steam engines are also brought into action from time to time.

Named after the Duke of Beaufort in 1818, Beaufort West is the largest town in the sheep farming district of the South-West Karoo. Its main claim to fame lies in the tale that one morning in 1849, herds of springbok, wildebeest, blestok, quagga and eland awakened the whole town. For three whole days they invaded the streets of the town, leaving the veld as though it had been devastated by fire.

Intrigued, I listened to one old timer relate how, in the past, establishing a train service through Beaufort West had been no easy task to accomplish. Protesters had warned of serious consequences if the iron horse was encouraged to compete with transport riders. The sight of the first locomotive roaring along at night, sparks flying, had terrified the primitive Hottentots, compelling many to leave, never to return. Scrutinising our blue and gold iron horse which proudly bore a handsome coat of arms and carried the inscription 'Blue Train' in Afrikaans and English, I could not help but think that it was still a commanding spectacle.

163

Cruising north, we breathed in the dry, invigorating air of the Karoo, leaving behind Nelsproot, and its state-owned sanatorium dedicated to the treatment of tuberculosis.

We stopped briefly at De Aar, one of South Africa's most important rail centres, almost halfway between Johannesburg and Cape Town. Meaning 'artery', its name is derived from the small spring nearby.

Further down the line, 130 kilometres south of Kimberley, lies Hopetown. It was here, in 1866, that the first diamond to be discovered in South Africa was unearthed. Three years later the famous gem, Star of South Africa, was purchased from Schalk van Niekerk for the princely sum of 22,000 rand.

On we travelled through Modder or Soft Mud river, a tributary of the Vaal, where the railway serves the township of Ritchie. Ten kilometres away at Magersfontein trench warfare first took place. Here three monuments were raised to commemorate Celtic, Boer and Scandinavian troops who fell in battle during the South African War.

Deep in the night we arrived at Kimberley, acclaimed for the magnitude of diamonds discovered since 1871 and the subsequent gold rush to the greatest man-made hole in the world. For me, the town had a more poignant significance.

Gazing down onto the busy platform, I recalled with nostalgia some of the tales related to me by a certain Dutchman not so very long ago. With great pride, he had recounted how his grandparents had withstood the siege of Kimberley, between October 1899 and February 1900. Enraptured, I had listened to graphic accounts of various precious stones, recovered from the Great Hole during the ensuing years. At the time, however, I was far more overwhelmed by the sparkle in his deep blue eyes which, for me, outshone any diamond on record.

Straining my eyes in the darkness, I still yearned to see the Big Hole, and diamond mining museum. Perhaps discover if the little shop, which he boasted had sold the world's most delicious pies, still existed. Now at last, when I was within stone-throwing distance of achieving my goal, I was unable to see beyond the end of the platform. 'Life is full of second chances,' I reminded myself philosophically.

At the point where the Vaal divides into fourteen streams, the train swept across the river. Bloemhof, the centre of the 1910 diamond rush, passed by unnoticed. Some of the old gravel mounds, I believe, can still be seen from the track, during daylight hours.

Affluent Klerksdorp on the Schoomsspruit received scant attention as it prepared for yet another busy day. Potchefstroom, steeped in history, the oldest town and once the capital of the Transvaal, fared little better.

Half asleep the following morning, with the thought of a cup of steaming hot coffee in mind, I followed Ian to the dining car. Once seated, however, the tantalising aroma which invaded my nostrils persuaded me to abandon my diet and join my husband in ordering an enormous cooked breakfast.

We entered the environs of Johannesburg through what could be described as a back door. The outlook of overgrown grassland and run down suburbs was decidedly bleak.

All too soon the Blue Train drew into Johannesburg's main line railway station, signalling that our journey of a lifetime was about to come to a halt.

Built on land that a century ago had housed a camp of tents, wagons and shacks, this centre of industry and commerce might still be nothing but an empty wilderness. It was by chance alone that a penniless prospector discovered the gold reef on land belonging to a widow Orsthuizen in 1886. Twelve months later, as the result of a gold rush, the area became known as Witwatersrand – Ridge of White Waters.

We had only one day left to spend in Johannesburg, as we were booked on a flight home early the next morning. With this in mind, we hired a car from a firm close by. Depositing our luggage in the boot, we made our way to the railway museum. Exhibited in the old station building, a fine display depicts the development of transport in South Africa since 1860. Being an admirer of Pierneef, I particularly looked forward to seeing some of his paintings also on display, but we had forgotten that it was a Sunday and, consequently, the museum was closed to the general public.

Casting aside our disappointment, we decided to make for the Carlton Centre to do some last minute shopping. Entering the complex, engraved, coloured footprints led us to a lift which carried us to the observation deck on the fiftieth floor. From here we had a panoramic view of that vibrant city.

Whilst browsing around the souvenir shops, I was soon tempted to part with my few remaining rand. That night courtesy of Ian's credit card, we treated ourselves to a sumptuous meal at La Bohème, which provided a romantic setting for our last evening in South Africa.

As our plane took off from Jan Smuts Airport the following morning, I gazed down fondly upon countless rows of tidy dwellings, neat gardens and numerous azure pools. The warning lights were eventually extinguished, replacing the strained silence with familiar sounds of safety belts and seats being readjusted. For a while I sat quietly, content to revel in some of those mystical moments of the past few days, reluctant to return to reality and face an uncertain future.

EPILOGUE

We returned to Zambia during the rainy season. Ian still managed to put in a full day at work, where an expensive computer system had been recently installed. To add to his troubles the accounts' package had developed a fault resulting in the loss of several important files. I had my own problems as I juggled with my swimming rosters, affected fairly frequently by sudden thunderstorms.

In July, Ian had to return to the clinic in Johannesburg for a check-up and as the swimming season had ended, I decided to accompany him. Before departing we organised a trip to Chichele Lodge in Luangwa National Park, with the intention of taking the children there during the school recess. Arriving in Johannesburg, we booked an apartment in Hillbrow, not far from the sky-high Post Office tower. Ian had to visit a hospital just a stone's throw away, where he was given daily doses of radium. Although the treatment made him feel extremely weak and tired, it never prevented him from returning, each day, to work at head office, situated not far from Soweto township, south-east of the city.

Hillbrow was a bustling, noisy locality – teeming with restaurants, shops, nightspots and theatres – where I always found plenty of places of interest to explore on my own. At the weekend, the two of us would visit one of the numerous flea markets which sprang up all over the place, or browse for a while in front of the Market Theatre, to be entertained by buskers of every description.

A week before Ian was due to complete his course of treatment I returned to Zambia as my sister was due to arrive from England for a month's vacation. Her visit also coincided with the return of the children from Grahamstown. It was a full car-load of passengers that greeted Ian the following week, when his flight from Johannesburg touched down at Ndola airport.

Unfortunately, a couple of days before we were due to leave for Luangwa, Ian took a turn for the worse and was unable to face the arduous journey. After much debate and soul searching on my part, it was decided – mainly for the children's benefit – that the rest of us would leave without him. The children were aware that their father had been unwell for some time, but knew none of the details. The doctor at the clinic in Kitwe came to our assistance and booked Ian into Luanshya Mine hospital for the week, where he was looked after by compassionate and caring staff.

As it turned out, leaving Ian behind was a wise decision, as the journey to Luangwa proved to be something of a nightmare. However, the same could not be said of the game park, which was every bit as exciting as we had been led to believe.

When we returned to the Copperbelt we held a braai as a joint celebration for Anthony and Fiona who both had birthdays around that time. While chatting over the fire's dying embers, Ian remarked that he intended to make a booking for the family to spend a long weekend at the Mosi-oa-Tunya, as he had a sudden yearning to see the Falls again.

This proved to be easier said than done, but after several set-backs, we arrived at our destination with Ian at the wheel of the Range Rover. Although he spent most of the time in the hotel suite, he did manage to visit his beloved Falls again. By then the border between Zambia and the new Zimbabwe had been reopened, so he was able to wander through the rain forest and revisit the small town of Victoria Falls which was so full of happy memories for us.

On the 27th September 1983, three weeks after all this took place, Ian died peacefully in his sleep following an operation in Johannesburg. We were reminded on numerous occasions that 'time is a great healer', and over the past 12 years this has indeed proved to be the case.

Although the children and I have now built a new and happy life overseas, I will never forget the wonderful times we spent in Africa, where I left not only my footprints but also my heart.

168